REAGAN ON LEADERSHIP

To John with leadership
With warm high
regards and
hopes for our work
together

James Strock
October 2000

REAGAN ON LEADERSHIP

Executive Lessons from the Great Communicator

JAMES M. STROCK

FORUM
An Imprint of Prima Publishing

To my family

© 1998 by Strock Enterprises, Inc.

FORUM is an imprint of Prima Publishing,
3875 Atherton Road, Rocklin, California 95765

PRIMA PUBLISHING and colophon
are registered trademarks of Prima Communications, Inc.

Library of Congress Cataloging-in-Publication Data
Strock, James M.
Reagan on leadership : executive lessons from the
Great Communicator / James M. Strock.
p. cm.
ISBN 0-7615-1336-1
1. Reagan, Ronald. 2. Political leadership—United States—History
20th century. 3. United States—Politics and government—1981–1989.
4. Reagan, Ronald—Quotations. I. Title.
E877.2.S77   1998
973.927'.092—dc21   98-11319
                                            CIP

98 99 00 01 02 HH 10 9 8 7 6 5 4 3 2 1
Printed in the United States of America

How to Order
Single copies may be ordered from Prima Publishing, P.O. Box 1260BK, Rocklin, CA 95677; telephone (916) 632-4400. Quantity discounts are also available. On your letterhead, include information concerning the intended use of the books and the number of books you wish to purchase.

Visit us online at http://www.primapublishing.com

CONTENTS

PREFACE

THERE IS MUCH discussion in America today about leadership—what it is, what it isn't, why and whether it matters. Some people who decry the absence of leadership—in business, government, or the nonprofit sector—draw solace from the hope that perhaps leadership is no longer as important as in the past.

This book is predicated on the conviction that leadership does matter and that it can be developed in part from the study of outstanding leaders. There can be no question that Ronald Reagan was a leader of the first rank. Whether one considers his accomplishments in achieving his vision or his legacy in terms of a changed public discourse, Reagan stands as one of the most consequential leaders of our time.

The British historian Lord Bryce observed, "Perhaps no form of government needs great leaders so much as democracy." From town hall meetings to the Congress to the White House to international forums, America has always relied upon large numbers of people assuming leadership roles.

Business enterprises of all types also rely on leadership. Small firms require it every bit as much as large corporations. In today's Information Age the opportunities for leadership have grown exponentially. Markets have become global: Information can be transferred instantaneously to buyers, sellers, distributors, competitors, and allies anywhere in the world.

Product cycles are accelerated beyond all experience. Traditional notions of management are manifestly inadequate in this environment. The rapid pace of change has even resulted in some private enterprises assuming roles generally understood to be within the province of the public sector. To the extent that multinational corporations in particular become "governments in merchants' clothing," the opportunities—and necessity—for leadership will further expand.

Ronald Reagan's relevance stems not merely from the fact that he foresaw and indeed helped bring about many of the changes whose consequences are being felt across our nation and the world. His *approach* to leadership merits close consideration. In some ways, Reagan's approach can be understood in the context of other major historical figures. There are aspects of leadership that are remarkably similar across time, place, and situation; this, of course, is a key reason why business writers so often rely on political and military examples. In other ways, his style is less familiar, though some of the aspects that his contemporaries found surprising may be more common in the years just ahead.

Reagan's unconventionality led some to underestimate him, though the powerful results he achieved have by now diminished his doubters' numbers considerably. I was among those who initially underestimated him. Observing his remarkable achievements, however, it dawned on me rather rapidly that the effectiveness of Reagan's approach made it worthy of sustained examination. He brings to mind the observation of the philosopher Alfred North Whitehead: "Men of different habits are not enemies; they are godsends."

This book is not an academic exercise. It is intended to be of practical value to individuals seeking or assuming leadership roles. As one who has had the opportunity to assist and advise chief executives, and later to lead large organizations myself, I have sought to identify and relate the essentials of Reagan's leadership style to others in similar situations.

Reagan on Leadership has four parts. The first examines the critical elements of Reagan's leadership approach: beginning with his vision and moving to his decisiveness, his negotiating style, his use of an "indirect" approach when direct action was foreclosed, his ability to make positive use of failure, and his unerring sense of timing.

The second section concerns management. Its premise is that management is a part of leadership; the two are necessarily related in practice. After considering Reagan's management philosophy, we will consider his practice of setting—and adhering to—a small number of fixed priorities. We then turn to delegation, the means by which an executive ensures that every member of a team best contributes to achieving priorities. We will also examine Reagan's skillful use of meetings, among the primary tools of any executive. This section makes clear the interrelationship between Reagan's vision-based leadership and the specifics of his management style.

The third section relates to communication, a vital element of successful leadership. In one sense Reagan—known as the "Great Communicator"—requires little introduction in this regard. This section isolates a small number of key communications concepts followed by Reagan, from which many other rules flow rather naturally.

The final section concerns Reagan's personal character, the self-management from which all other leadership skills ultimately arise. A consequential leader, in any endeavor, generally comes to personify the vision he seeks to actualize. Ultimately, the heedlessness of self that is the hallmark of such leaders is based upon highly developed, generally recognized personal traits that are as relevant in the Information Age as the Agriculture Age.

Following each chapter is a series of principles. Readers will note that some are drawn directly from Reagan quotations, while others are derived from his practices. Unlike some other prominent leaders with readily recognizable leadership styles, such as Theodore Roosevelt (whose career included membership on the U.S. Civil Service Commission), Reagan did not speak or write in great detail about his approach. Nonetheless, his practices followed identifiable, repeating patterns.

Finally, a linguistic note. A small difficulty in contemporary written English is the unsettled state of the tradition of using "he" and "his" as universal, encompassing both male and female genders. Expedients such as repeating "he or she" are awkward for a writer and distracting for a reader. For ease of expression, in the absence of an agreed successor, I have chosen to use the male pronouns in the traditional, universal sense.

ACKNOWLEDGMENTS

THOUGH WRITING APPEARS to be a solitary enterprise, it provides constant reminders of one's debts to others. Without implicating others in conclusions with which they may disagree, I would nonetheless like to acknowledge some of the more conspicuous debts.

Special thanks are due to the outstanding individuals who graciously took time from their own crowded hours to share memories of and reflections on Ronald Reagan's leadership. These include Dr. Martin Anderson, Douglas L. Bailey, Hon. Howard H. Baker Jr., William F. Buckley Jr., Michael K. Deaver, Craig L. Fuller, Peter Hannaford, Kenneth L. Khachigian, Hon. Edwin Meese III, Joseph D. Rodota Jr., Hon. George P. Shultz, Dr. Kevin Starr, Kirk West, Robert White, and Hon. Pete Wilson.

I would also like to acknowledge intellectual debts that go further than can be conveyed by footnotes. Every individual seeking to learn about Ronald Reagan owes a particular debt to journalist Lou Cannon. His articles and books on Reagan are an indispensable resource. The analysis of leadership and management in this book explores veins opened in the writings of Warren Bennis, James MacGregor Burns, Stephen Covey, and Peter Drucker. The work of Richard E. Neustadt, for whom I am proud to have worked as a teaching assistant nearly two decades ago, provided a valuable perspective against which to consider Reagan's approach to the presidency.

Erin Schiller of the Pacific Research Institute in San Francisco provided excellent research assistance. The staff at the Ronald Reagan Presidential Library were helpful in providing access to archival records. Special thanks are owed to Lynda L. Schuler of the Reagan Foundation for help and encouragement throughout the project. Steven Martin, Jennifer Fox, and Hilary Powers of Prima Publishing repeatedly exhibited skill as well as patience in editing a first-time author. Additional thanks are owed to Joachim Baer, Rachel and Charles Bernheim, Michael Epperson, Todd Foley, Steven Hayward, Terry Johnston, George Montgomery, Bonita Morgan, Jürgen Resch, Brian Runkel, Fr. John Schlegel, Lou Smallwood, Richard Norton Smith, and Michael Zickerick.

In dedicating this book to my family, I would like to express particular thanks to my late grandfather James L. Tenney, who first taught me about leadership, and my late father, James M. Strock, who imparted a love for books and writing.

INTRODUCTION

JANUARY 20, 1981

THE EARLY MORNING hours were cloudy and cold. All across Washington, preparations for the transfer of power to the president-elect, Ronald Reagan, were busily under way. Following an evening of preinaugural celebrations, the city was bracing for inaugural ceremonies of a style—critics would say lavishness—recalling an earlier time, particularly the Hollywood-influenced extravaganza for John F. Kennedy in 1961.

No one was busier than the outgoing president, Jimmy Carter. He had been in his office all day and all night over the prior 48 hours. He wore the familiar cardigan sweater, which he had offered as an example of how to save energy in a televised address to the nation earlier in his term. The president's extraordinary hands-on approach had a cost: "I needed to be constantly alert, but there were periods when I realized I was not at my best." Nonetheless, Carter hoped that his final burst of bustle would allow him to leave office on a high note:

bringing home the 52 American hostages held in Iran since November 4, 1979.

Keeping meticulous handwritten notes on a pad, beginning at 1:50 A.M. on Tuesday morning, President Carter recorded every detail of the progress and setbacks in his final day of office. The "big grandfather clock by the door" of the Oval Office moved with remorseless, heedless speed and finality. Finally, at 6:35 A.M., Carter received a telephone call from his primary negotiator, notifying him that final arrangements for the release of the hostages had been signed moments before.

At last Carter could grasp the chance of redemption from his decline in public estimation during his single term of office. His hard work, his ceaseless personal attention to the details of the lives, families, and well-being of the hostages—even to the doomed military rescue attempt that ended tragically with American airpower splayed in the desert—would be rewarded. His speechwriters went to work preparing a televised address that Carter planned to deliver before the inauguration ceremonies later in the morning.

Shortly before 7:00 A.M., President Carter placed a telephone call to President-Elect Reagan. Reagan, as is customary, was staying across Pennsylvania Avenue, in shouting distance from the White House, at the official guest house, Blair House.

Reagan was not available.

An aide reported to Carter that the call was intercepted by Reagan staff, who explained that the one-time actor "had had a long night, was sleeping, and was not to be disturbed."

"You're kidding," an incredulous Carter replied.

"No, sir, I'm not."

Like a punctilious grade-school student making notes for a teacher, Carter took pen to paper, evidently anxious that history not miss this outrageous incident. "I place a call to Governor Reagan to give him the good news, and am informed that he prefers not to be disturbed, but that he may call back later. I respond that I will call him when the hostages are released."

Across the street, the incoming president, having achieved the most powerful elective office in the world, making it to the top of what the British call "the greasy pole" of political advancement, was taking it all in stride. In fact, he was in bed.

As the clock moved past eight, Reagan's close aide Michael Deaver sought out the prospective first couple:

> When I walked in, Nancy was getting her hair done. I said, "Where's the governor?"
>
> Without moving her head, she said, "I guess he's still in bed."
>
> "In bed," I repeated. "If it was me, if I was about to become president of the United States, I don't think I'd still be asleep at nine o'clock on the morning of my swearing in."
>
> I opened the door to the bedroom. It was pitch-dark, the curtains still drawn, and I could barely make out a heap of blankets in the middle of the bed. I said, "Governor?"
>
> "Yeah?"
>
> "It's nine o'clock."
>
> "Yeah?"
>
> "Well, you're going to be inaugurated in two hours."
>
> "Does that mean I have to get up?"

Reagan soon returned the president's call. Carter reported that the hostage release was imminent, and the planes to return them home were on the runway in Teheran, poised for takeoff.

At 9:45, Carter received another telephone update from his hostage release negotiator in the Middle East: "Takeoff is not imminent, but I can state for certain that it will be before noon."

Still with no resolution, the clock raced toward 11:00, when Governor and Mrs. Reagan would arrive at the White House for the customary coffee meeting of the outgoing and incoming president. At 10:45 Carter's wife, Rosalynn, urged him to head to the family quarters of the White House, to shave and dress. Although Carter had worn a plain business suit for his own inaugural four years earlier, for today he had rented a formal morning suit to match Reagan's.

Carter, by his own account, was "discouraged and almost exhausted." He later noted, "As I looked at myself in the mirror, I wondered if I had aged so much as President or whether I was just exhausted" from staying in his office nonstop during the preceding few days.

At the appointed time Reagan entered the White House. Well rested, doubtless in his customary buoyant, jaunty, somewhat cheeky manner, he made a marked contrast to his younger, defeated, weary, embittered predecessor. At nearly 70, the oldest man to take the presidential oath the first time, Ronald Reagan looked like . . . a movie star. Carter's relative condition had not gone unnoticed. Reagan later asked aide Deaver: "Did you get a look at Carter?" Deaver observed that Carter's face was "absolutely ashen," and "he had dark circles under his eyes and it was obvious he had not slept all night."

After eleven the two leaders entered the presidential limousine for the ride down Pennsylvania Avenue from the White House to the Capitol. Photographs of the two together on that morning show what may be the most uncomfortable inaugural pairing since Herbert Hoover gave way to Franklin Roosevelt in March 1933. Carter's pursed lips conveyed a barely disguised contempt for Reagan, much as Hoover's stony countenance, uncreased by goodwill or pleasantry, served as an unintended backdrop for Americans looking for hope in FDR's unperturbed, unstoppable smile.

Hoover resented Roosevelt's unwillingness to work with him during the long transitional interregnum between the 1932 election and the inaugural, as public despair deepened in the face of the unprecedented Great Depression. Similarly, Carter could not understand Reagan's apparent lack of interest in the affairs of government.

Inside the Capitol, Carter continued to monitor the hostage situation, hopeful that the planes on the runway in Teheran would take off with their precious cargo before noon, in his final moments as president. As the minutes passed, the planes remained at the end of the runway, tantalizingly close, but still not airborne.

As President Carter began to make his way to the inaugural platform, he instructed an aide to immediately notify him should the hostages be released before noon. Carter would then be able to announce their release as his valedictory statement to the American people.

Reagan, despite his known aversion for Carter, was cooperative. Showing grace as he prepared to take the podium and the mantle of office, Reagan told an aide: "I have a feeling they are going to get the hostages back. If it happens, even during my address, I want you to tell me. Slip me a note. Interrupt me. Because if it happens, I want you to bring Carter up to the platform. I think it is outrageous that they are treating this president this way."

The hostages began taking off at 12:33 P.M. President Reagan made the announcement at lunch. As Reagan noted in his memoirs, "Jimmy Carter was already on his way to Georgia, and my heart went out to him: I wished he had had the chance to make that announcement."

REAGAN'S FIRST DAY as president illustrated certain aspects of his approach to leadership. He was single-mindedly focused on what he considered his top priority for that day: presenting his vision in his inaugural address. In being unavailable for Carter's early-morning telephone call, Reagan trusted his staff's judgment to protect him from an interruption of sleep that would have served no purpose in achieving the release of the hostages (he had already done all he could on that score) but could have made him less rested as he approached one of the most important speeches of his life. Rather than laziness, this could be interpreted as wise discipline.

He also evinced a light touch of humor and unusual grace in dealing with his predecessor under trying circumstances. This cannot have come easily. Carter viciously struck at one of Reagan's rawest nerves in the late campaign, all but directly calling him a racist. In the same vein, several days prior to the inauguration the Carters turned the Reagans over to White House staff for their tour of the family quarters—an act that the Californians understandably took as "an affront."

Reagan recognized that he had much larger concerns: His audience that day was primarily the American people, secondarily the people of the world. He would begin to restore dignity of office through his return to traditional formal dress; he offered encouragement to Americans shaken by a decade of uncertainty by his readily apparent confidence and optimism. If Reagan could assume the American presidency with such assurance, given the recent history of his predecessors and the many domestic and international challenges at his doorstep, surely the rest of us could handle our own difficult if more mundane challenges. Watching the sun break through the clouds as Reagan stepped up to take the oath of office, Americans could already see that a new kind of leadership was coming.

It is important to recall that President Carter's ravaged visage exemplified the terrible price in health and well-being paid by most recent presidents. Magazines have run "before and after" photographs showing the vibrant, healthful, enthusiastic new presidents entering office, juxtaposed with the physical ruins who leave. By 1981, many Americans had never known a successful presidency. John Kennedy died by an assassin's bullet after less than three years in office. Lyndon Johnson, who initially dominated the Washington scene as few presidents ever had, rapidly lost his way and left office an embittered, scorned, lonely, and prematurely aged figure. Richard Nixon, broken by his own misjudgments and malfeasance, left one step ahead of prosecutors. Gerald Ford, surely one of the kindest gentlemen ever to inhabit the White House, never seemed to have a sure hold on the levers of power.

Carter, eager to lead America beyond the traumas of recent years, brought a commendable determination to the office, combined with a distinctive dedication to detail. When he was governor it was said that he prided himself on reading every bill he would sign; as president he would show a mastery of technical issues often matching that of specialists. His work habits were legendary—it is likely that no president spent longer hours at his desk.

For all his dedication, Carter marked the spot whenever the terms *hapless* and *leader* came together. The unfinished challenges left for his successor were, to say the least, daunting.

Across the world, regimes acting in the name of Marxist ideology, for all of its manifest failures, were ascendant. In Southeast Asia, Vietnam, Laos, and Cambodia had succumbed. The Soviet Union invaded Afghanistan. Nicaragua was ruled by leftist gangsters, and El Salvador appeared poised for a similar fate. In Africa, Robert Mugabe installed one-party rule in the new Zimbabwe, following the exit of the British from the colonial remnant, Rhodesia. America's irresolution in the face of this baleful trend—and its incapacity to shape events—was perhaps most aptly symbolized by the Iranian hostage saga.

The domestic economy was in turmoil. In 1980 inflation was rising at an annual rate of 12 percent, even as the unemployment rate rose above 7 percent. Real wages—taking taxes into account—were plunging at a dizzying rate. The continuing natural gas and oil shortages of the end of the decade, traceable to the supply shocks administered by the oil-exporting nations earlier, illustrated the interconnection between uncertainty at home and uncertainty abroad.

Perhaps most threatening was the decline in confidence in public institutions and leadership. No one could take heart in the departure from power of yet another president, broken by the demands of the office. President Carter, unable to lead the nation or indeed his administration despite his diligent efforts, found the cause in a "crisis of confidence"—later labeled a "malaise" by commentators—afflicting the American people. Added to the corrosive absence of trust engendered by the establishment's handling of the Vietnam conflict and the Watergate scandals, this apparent shifting of the blame from the leaders to the people was undermining the distinctively American faith that the future held a better life for their children than themselves.

Ronald Reagan changed all this—and more. When he left office after eight years, America's economy was again the envy, and the engine, of the entire world. Inflation was down, employment was up, international trade was expanding. The influence of his policies was seen not only in the attractive example set, but also in the forces it unleashed. For example, in lowering the top income tax rates from 70 percent to 28 percent, Reagan's policies led other nations in the same direction, to prevent an accelerating flight of capital from their own economies to America's.

The Cold War with the Soviet Union, which had dominated American foreign policy since the end of the Second World War—and greatly affected life at home, as well—was "won." The first nuclear arms reduction treaty (as opposed to the prior treaties, which limited or stabilized nuclear arsenals) was signed. The Soviet Union, publicly lacerated as the "Evil

Empire" by President Reagan, was brought to the brink of the dissolution that finally came to pass in 1989–91.

Above all, Reagan restored America's belief in itself. He proved conclusively that the presidency could be successfully handled. To the surprise of many, this conservative restored public faith in the competence of government. He left office with record-high approval ratings from the public. The oldest man to hold the office of president had a unique bond with the young: 87 percent of people from 18 to 29 years old approved of Reagan "as a person." Fully 57 percent of Americans expressed the view that Reagan would be regarded as an outstanding or above-average president, including 70 percent of young people.

The enduring value of Reagan's legacy is seen not only in the lasting consequences of his accomplishments, but in the political dialogue he altered. Like his idol Franklin D. Roosevelt, Reagan understood that if he could alter the political discussion, policy would inevitably continue to follow the new course. Though many of Reagan's conservative Republican supporters may not have been pleased by Democrat Bill Clinton's two presidential election victories, they should recognize that his unabashed effort to mimic the "Great Communicator" is indicative of a larger victory.

After an initial foray into traditional New Deal governance, most notably his proposal of a centralized national health care plan to be run from Washington, Clinton found himself without public support—and soon without a congressional majority. Approaching the 1996 election from a position of vulnerability, Clinton's staff seized upon the Reagan example to the greatest possible extent. He reportedly studied films of Reagan in various settings, to learn what a president should act like in public. He adopted Reaganite rhetoric—seeing an optimistic future in an "age of possibility," calling for a balanced federal budget, urging respect for and protection of middle American values, and promoting a strong national defense. Clinton's support for congressional passage of the North American Free Trade Agreement, arguably the most significant act of his presidency, helped fulfill Reagan's vision of the Americas united by trade. Ultimately, the same president who had failed in what would have been the greatest expansion of government power of the decade would eventually follow Reagan's rhetoric to its inevitable conclusion, exclaiming, "The age of Big Government is over."

This kind of change in the political discussion has consequences, not only on the great policy decisions but also on the many smaller decisions made with reference to it. More than two decades ago, President Richard Nixon astounded his supporters and opponents alike, turning his back on nearly 40 years of Republican opposition to the fundamental economic tenets of Franklin Roosevelt's New Deal. Referring to John Maynard Keynes, the late English intellectual whose theories were invoked by liberal economists, he declared: "We are all Keynesians now."

As the 20th century comes to a close, when we look at America—our priorities at home and abroad, the means applied to make change, and the terms of public debate—it is clear that we are all "Reaganites" now.

IN HIS AUTOBIOGRAPHY, *An American Life*, Reagan wrote lovingly about his California retreat, Rancho del Cielo. Recounting his close relationship with the Secret Service agents who protected him, he told a story about his use of guns:

> I've never liked hunting, simply killing an animal for the pleasure of it, but I have always enjoyed and collected unusual guns; I love target shooting, and have always kept a gun for protection at home. As I had done when I was governor, I sometimes did some

target shooting with the Secret Service agents who accompanied us to the ranch, and occasionally managed to amaze them with my marksmanship. We have a small pond on the ranch that sometimes attracts small black snakes, and every now and then, one would stick its head up out of the water for a second or two. After I'd see one, I'd go into the house and come back with a .38 revolver, go into a little crouch, and wait for the next snake to rise up. Then I'd shoot.

Well, since I was thirty feet or more from the lake, the Secret Service agents were shocked that I was able to hit the snake every time. They'd shake their heads and say to each other, *"How the hell does he do it?"*

Like the Secret Service agents, many others have seen Reagan accomplish extraordinary things and have been mystified as to how he did it. Some have concluded that Reagan had nothing to do with whatever accomplishments emanated from the organizations he led. One book, *The Acting President* by Bob Schieffer and Gary Paul Gates, concluded: "Ronald Reagan had very little to do with his administration and the issues that came before it."

Several of Reagan's former aides sought to give credence to the notion that he was merely stage-managed by others—most notably, his former aides. Following his admittedly bitter departure from the Reagan administration, former treasury secretary and chief of staff Donald Regan wrote:

There was no design for leadership. There was no inventory of national priorities, no philosophical consensus on which policy was based, no system for carrying a problem that subordinates could not solve to the President for final decision, no provision for the confidentiality without which no friendship, no marriage, no business, and certainly no Presidency can function. It seemed to me, after four years of living in an environment in which policy seemed to be made on the basis of a belief in public opinion that amounted to superstition, that the Presidency was in need of sound management advice.

In his outstanding book, *Revolution,* long-time Reagan adviser Martin Anderson responded tellingly to such critics:

At first, this characterization of Ronald Reagan struck me as preposterous. Were serious people actually suggesting that someone who was that slow-witted and irresponsible could get elected governor of California, our largest state, govern successfully for four years under the critical eye of the California press corps, get reelected and serve successfully for four more years, come within an eyelash of wresting the Republican party nomination from a sitting president in 1976, win that nomination in 1980, get elected president of the United States by beating an incumbent president, serve successfully for four years under the intense scrutiny of the national and the international press corps—and then get reelected by one of the largest margins in United States history?

Anderson added that such a person would have "had to be the luckiest man ever to walk on this good earth. . . . No one is that lucky."

This book will argue that Reagan's leadership and management style, while original in some aspects and perhaps singular in a few, has components that can be isolated, studied, and applied by others. Whether one aspires to leadership in a large corporation, as an entrepreneur, in a nonprofit organization, or in government, Reagan offers lessons that can add value.

While there are obvious differences in public, private, and nonprofit organizations, there is also much overlap in the area of leadership. It is no accident that Peter Drucker, perhaps the most respected authority on management of this era, used many examples from political leadership as well as corporations in his important book *The Effective Executive*. This has an additional resonance in considering Reagan, who strongly believed in the superiority of private enterprise over public organizations in terms of achieving results.

In the case of the Secret Service agents amazed by his rare marksmanship, Reagan eventually revealed his approach: "What they didn't know was that my pistol was loaded with shells containing bird shot—like a shot gun—instead of a conventional slug. I kept my secret for a while, but finally decided to fess up and tell them about the bird shot."

Reagan was not publicly introspective. It is difficult to imagine his telling the rest of us about his leadership and management style in the way in which he revealed his use of bird shot to the agents. Nonetheless, the record of his career, the commentary of others, and his own words lay out a clear, discernible approach to leadership.

As with other great leaders, Reagan's approach is ultimately based on the power of a compelling vision. And as one expects of the man who came to be called the "Great Communicator," Reagan was uniquely effective in communicating his vision through all available media—radio, movies, television—and before live audiences both large and small.

To implement his vision, Reagan established a series of management and personnel practices that proved remarkably successful in his tenure as governor of California and later in the White House. The Iran-Contra debacle of 1987 was the lone great exception; it was the result of deviating from the approach that had served Reagan so well in the past. What is more, it occasioned yet another lesson of broad application: how to handle a crisis or failure.

Perhaps because of his natural gifts—including the improbable combination of a telegenic and handsome face, a manifestly strong body, a melodious voice, and a photographic memory—some people believe him to be a "oner" from whom there is little to be learned. In a sense, he was of course unique—as is everyone. And the time and place in which he rose to leadership are now greatly changed. But if the precise gifts that set Reagan apart were really the only important ones, surely he would have ushered in a golden age of movie actors in public life.

What may be more unusual about Reagan were the traits of character that he exhibited throughout his career. His courage, authenticity, empathy, grace, discipline, perseverance, humility, and sense of dignity were also essential to his accomplishments as a leader. Character is indeed an achievement, but it is one to which all can aspire; the character of a specific leader is something others can learn from.

Reagan's example suggests an additional set of lessons of particular relevance today and in the coming years. We all recognize him as a leading advocate of what are now called "traditional values," and he often exhibited an unapologetic admiration for the ways of an older, pre–World War II America. Nonetheless, Reagan's own career was anything but conventional. After working as a radio announcer, he became a motion picture actor. He also served as president of a labor union and was an early participant in the then-risky (or so thought many movie actors) medium of television. He spent considerable time, in various capacities through his working life, as a professional public speaker. He was also a successful radio commentator on current events in the 1970s, presaging the later emergence of "talk radio."

At the age of 55, with no prior experience in government, Reagan's first electoral campaign was for the governorship of California. What is more, his background as an actor was viewed suspiciously by some, contemptuously by others. His opponent, a hitherto successful conventional politician whom he ultimately defeated handily, even ran television advertisements highlighting this supposedly "suspect" lack of credentials. Finding that his acting skills could give him an advantage as a campaigner, Reagan rapidly overcame similar initial doubts about his ability to perform as chief executive of the world's seventh-largest economy.

Later, in his third presidential campaign in 1980, Reagan faced another, potentially more damaging deviation from conventional expectation: his advanced age. Through skill and discipline, he overcame this supposed disadvantage as well.

Anyone who has sought or achieved a position while being in some way "different" from what is customary—whether by racial or ethnic heritage, gender, age, or disability, or bereft of expected experience or credentials—will find much to apply from Reagan's example. Indeed, given the increasing opportunities for leadership in the Information Age, combined with the changing demographics of the United States in the next generation, this may eventually be viewed as one of Reagan's more surprising, important, and durable legacies.

PART 1

LEADERSHIP

The greatest leader is not necessarily the one who does the greatest
things; he is the one who gets the people to do the greatest things.
—RONALD REAGAN

"Fail to honor people, they will fail to honor you."
But of a Great Leader, when his work is done, his aim fulfilled,
the people will all say, "We did this ourselves."
—LAO-TZU, CIRCA 6TH CENTURY B.C.

CHAPTER 1

CRAFT A COMPELLING VISION

———◆———

"The most important thing is to have the vision.
The next is to grasp and hold it. You must see and feel
what you are thinking. You must see it and grasp it."
—RONALD REAGAN, QUOTING SERGEI EISENSTEIN,
SOVIET FILMMAKER, TO MOSCOW AUDIENCE,
MAY 31, 1988

Where there is no vision, the people perish.
—PROVERBS 29:18

FIRST THERE IS A VISION.

One person, standing apart from others, presumes to point the way the group should move into the future. He stands, in a sense, between the group and the future, reporting what is ahead and explaining its significance to the rest. If the vision is understandable, credible, shared, and compelling, the people will join the leader and move forward together.

Every enterprise—beginning a business, starting a family, running a division within a company, teaching a class, or serving as a platoon commander in the military, to name a few—is based upon such a vision.

In Seattle, Howard Schultz wondered why American neighborhoods were not enriched by the presence of traditional conversational, family-oriented, romantic coffee bars like those he had observed and come to love in Europe. His vision, combining a high-quality product with an atmosphere where people could comfortably gather throughout the day, became the basis for the remarkable Starbucks chain.

Like missionaries of old, Microsoft leaders Bill Gates and Steve Ballmer have tirelessly offered a vision of a future in which individuals are empowered through the use of personal computers. Their goal is nothing less than a computer on every desk and in every home. Whether one is writing a book, starting a business, planning a vacation, or studying for school, this remarkable tool is tangibly changing lives for the better.

Charles Schwab glimpsed the future that would result from the convergence of the Information Age with the traditional, outwardly arcane and clubby ways of Wall Street. On the strength of this insight, he built a financial services powerhouse offering individuals the opportunity to manage their own investments, disseminating information once limited to professionals. His corporate vision: "We believe that everyone can take control of their financial future."

These business leaders, while different in many ways, are similar in their reliance on a compelling vision. In their best-selling book *Leaders,* Warren Bennis and Burt Nanus, having systematically studied leadership in numerous organizational settings, state unequivocally: "We cannot exaggerate the significance of a strong determination to achieve a goal or realize a vision—a conviction, even a passion." They add, "If there is a spark of genius in the leadership function at all, it must lie in this transcending ability, a kind of magic, to assemble—out of all the variety of images, signals, forecasts and alternatives—a clearly articulated vision of the future that is at once simple, easily understood, clearly desirable, and energizing."

Nowhere is the power of vision more evident than in the realm of politics. Though there are differences separating the political realm from private life, on the significance of vision they are as one. As in business, the political leaders of greatest consequence have been those with the most compelling visions.

George Washington was able to articulate and symbolize the vision of an independent, historically unique America. Washington was indeed "the indispensable man" whose actions established the presidency as well as many traditions and practices of leadership that we now take for granted. He brought together the American people, relying on the assistance of an unmatched group of citizens committed to political life, ranging from Jefferson and Adams to Madison and Hamilton. Their leadership task: to demonstrate for the first time in history that a republic of such geographic breadth and relatively large population could survive, prosper, adapt, and become a beacon to the world.

Later, as America was riven by the Civil War, unable to continue to contain the contradiction of slavery within our constitutional structure, Abraham Lincoln looked back to the Declaration of Independence for the connecting principles that would bind us together. Lincoln's vision of *the* United States, rather than *these* United States, prevailed.

One hundred years later Dr. Martin Luther King Jr. updated the American story with his dream: "that my four little children will one day live in a nation where they will not be judged by the color of their skin, but by the content of their character." Speaking to a large crowd from the base of the Lincoln Memorial—but cognizant that his audience included the American people as a whole—King made his message irresistible, another leader in another time standing on the strong edifice of the Declaration of Independence.

The significance of vision goes to the core of leadership. Indeed leadership is inseparable from vision. One can imagine a leader with many flaws, but if there is a compelling vision, such an individual may nonetheless earn widespread allegiance and support. In the absence of a compelling vision, even the most attractive person one might imagine—combining the looks of a fashion model, the reassuring personality of the television talk show host, the voice of a radio announcer, the knowledge of a professor, all presented with the unassuming modesty of a saint—would likely not be acknowledged as a leader.

Vision links the present to the future through the person of the leader. It also links the role of the leader—who provides general, strategic direction—to that of the manager who seeks to implement the vision in the context of day-to-day decision making. (The manager, of course, may also serve as a leader of his part of the larger organization). A vision that is widely understood and can be translated into action can empower large numbers of people. Decision making can thus be broadly dispersed and initiative sparked at many levels.

To achieve maximum force, a vision should be *simple*. Through force of repetition it can be easily remembered; by its nature it can be widely applied. It should also be *flexible*. A vision based upon principle might hold within it various approaches or policies, some of which might succeed while others fail, some of which might appear to be contradictory. The vision should also be *consistent with the values and history of the group*. If achievement of a vision is particularly daring or difficult, this may be all the more significant. To the extent that the leader can credibly *personify the vision*, embody it in his actions both large and small, its effectiveness can be further enhanced. If the vision is to encompass large numbers of people it must be *inclusive* rather than exclusive. If the vision is to inspire trust, it must be adhered to with *constancy*. It must create a shared, credible, contagious *optimism*, making people confident that their future can be better than the present, justifying their sacrifices, risks, or sense of uncertainty in the face of change.

Ronald Reagan, to an extent unequaled in recent American history, achieved elective office and then governed with the power of a vision that met all these criteria. His vision helped bring to a close the great totalitarian challenge to freedom that scarred most of the 20th century. His unshakable belief in the power of the individual and in the applicability of "American values" throughout the world points the way as we enter the new millennium.

REAGAN'S CONSISTENT VISION

At the heart of our message should be five simple familiar words.
No big economic theories. No sermons on political philosophy. Just
five short words: family, work, neighborhood, freedom, peace.
—RONALD REAGAN, 1980

There are a few leaders whose very names come to represent the vision for which they stand. By including the term "Reaganism," the *Oxford English Dictionary* bestowed this distinction on Ronald Reagan.

Reagan's vision was remarkably consistent throughout his career, ranging from his early years as a committed liberal to his middle and later years as one of the most famous conservatives in America and the world. His fundamental belief was in freedom of the individual—and in the one nation that was built around its pursuit. As he said during his 1984 reelection campaign: "Ours is the land of the free because it is the home of the brave. America's future will always be great because our nation will always be strong. And our nation will be strong because our people will be free. And our people will be free because we will be united, one people under God, with liberty and justice for all." Reagan would identify and challenge any threat to that freedom—at one time from corporate power, later from overweening domestic government and ultimately from the threat of a nuclear Armageddon posed by the Soviet Union.

During his presidency, his actions were constantly aimed toward actualizing the principles encompassed by the five central concepts of his vision: family, work, neighborhood, freedom, and peace.

Family

The love and common sense of purpose that unites families is one of the most powerful glues on earth and . . . it can help them overcome the greatest of adversities. . . . I have always wondered at this American marvel, the great energy of the human soul that drives people to better themselves and improve the fortunes of their families and communities. I know of no greater force on earth.
—RONALD REAGAN

The family was the foundation of Reagan's vision for America. As he explained to Soviet students in 1988, "Democracy is less a system of government than it is a system to keep government limited, unintrusive; a system of constraints on power to keep politics and government secondary to the important things in life, the true sources of value found only in family and faith." With an eye toward the many functions successfully handled by families, he sought to limit government regulation that could weaken them: "We fear that government may be powerful enough to destroy families; we know that it is not powerful enough to replace them."

In Reagan's view, cutting taxation and regulation was important not only as a means of restoring overall economic prosperity, but also as a means of strengthening the family unit. Lower taxes and less economic regulation would mean more money left in the hands of families to use as they saw fit. Changes in "social" regulation could also limit the encroachment of government bureaucracies into moral issues he believed best handled by families. Thus, for example, he sought to ensure that parents would be notified when their school-aged children sought contraception assistance from clinics receiving federal funding.

Work

No power of government is as formidable a force for good as the creativity and entrepreneurial drive of the American people.
—RONALD REAGAN

Like many others of his generation, Reagan was indelibly marked by the scars of the unexpected, unremitting privation that gripped America during the Great Depression of the 1930s. Unlike the Baby Boom generation (born in the aftermath of World War II through the early 1960s), Reagan's generation always sensed a fragility in economic prosperity; they could take nothing for granted. Reagan's down-to-earth focus on work as the source of the basic material goods that made it possible to care for oneself and one's family served him well when he sought the presidency during the economic distress of the late 1970s and early 1980s.

To a great extent Reagan drew conclusions about economics generally from his own personal experiences in the working world. In an era when many focused on large, impersonal

economic forces and the ability of government to plan, Reagan
saw economics in terms of individuals. In the terms of aca-
demics, he sought answers more from "microeconomics" than
from "macroeconomics." This meant that his vision did not
require translation to individuals; it relied on individuals.
Reagan contrasted his approach with that of his political
opponents in the 1980 election: "Our economy was one of the
great wonders of the world. It didn't need master planners. It
worked because it operated on principles of freedom, millions
of people going about their daily business and making free
decisions how they wanted to work and live, how they wanted
to spend their money, while reaping the rewards of their individual labor." He presented a choice:

> You see, we can either have an economy that puts the private
> citizen at the center—the consumer, the worker, the entrepre-
> neur—and lets each individual be the judge of what to buy or
> sell, where to work, where to invest, and what to create. Or we
> can put the government at the center of the economy and let the
> bureaucrats and politicians call the balls and strikes and decide
> who's out of business, or who will get the big contract and be
> home free.

Neighborhood

*This is the backbone of our country: Americans helping
themselves and each other. Reaching out and finding solutions—
solutions that government and huge institutions can't find.*
—RONALD REAGAN

Believing in the essential goodness of people, Reagan set great
store by the ability of individuals to look out for one another
in their own communities. Shorn of anonymity, there they

were likely to do the right things for themselves and others. He had seen this in Dixon, Illinois, the town in which he grew up:

> Almost everyone knew one another, and because they knew one another, they tended to care about each other. If a family down the street had a crisis—a death or serious illness—a neighbor brought them dinner that night. If a farmer lost his barn to a fire, his friends would pitch in and help him rebuild it. At church, you prayed side by side with your neighbors, and if things were going wrong for them, you prayed for them—and knew they'd pray for you if things went wrong for you.

Insofar as neighborhood institutions could provide succor for those in need, the role of government—and what Reagan saw as its attendant risks—could be limited. Reagan said that in addition to secular charitable institutions, he saw a particular role for religious institutions:

> There is a role for churches and temples . . . just as there has been throughout our history. They were once the center of community activity, the primary source of help for the less fortunate, with the churches that ran orphanages, homes for the elderly, other vital services. As late as 1935, at the depth of the Great Depression, a substantial portion of all charity was sponsored by religious institutions. And today, as we all know, the field seems to have been co-opted by government.

In Reagan's view, the efforts of individuals to assist others were more likely to succeed than government programs, no matter how well intentioned. Based in part on his own observations during the Great Depression—when his father ran a federal New Deal program in Dixon, the local Works Progress Administration—Reagan later concluded, "The first rule of bureaucracy is to protect the bureaucracy. If the people running a welfare program had let their clientele find other ways

of making a living, that would have reduced their importance
and their budget.

Freedom

> *All of these things—learning to control the government,*
> *limiting the amount of money it can take from us, protecting*
> *our country through a strong defense—all of these things*
> *revolve around one word, and that word is "freedom."*
> —RONALD REAGAN

> *A man wrote me and said: "You can go to live in France, but*
> *you cannot become a Frenchman. You can go to live in Germany*
> *or Turkey or Japan, but you cannot become a German, a Turk,*
> *or a Japanese. But anyone, from any corner of the Earth, can*
> *come to live in America and become an American."*
> —RONALD REAGAN

The theme that runs like a golden thread through Reagan's life
is his advocacy for freedom. He believed that moral and economic progress was based on the achievements of individuals
who believe in themselves, because they have faith in God.

According to Reagan's vision, America has a unique place
in the history of the world. That position is not because of
our natural resources or any inherent characteristic of our
people; it arises from our religious origins: "This blessed land
was set apart in a very special way, a country created by men
and women who came here not in search of Gold, but in
search of God. They would be a free people, living under the
law with faith in their Maker and their future."

Throughout his career as governor of California and
through his two terms as president, Reagan spoke of America

as the "shining city on a hill." Leaving the White House in 1989, he spoke of John Winthrop, the author of that vision: "What he imagined was important because he was an early freedom man . . . like the other Pilgrims, he was looking for a home that would be free." He continued:

> I've spoken of the shining city all my political life, but I don't know if I ever quite communicated what I saw when I said it. But in my mind it was a tall proud city built on rocks stronger than oceans, wind-swept, God-blessed, and teeming with people of all kinds living in harmony and peace, a city with free ports that hummed with commerce and creativity, and if there had to be city walls, the walls had doors and the doors were open to anyone with the will and the heart to get here.

Reagan's vision was extraordinarily inclusive—indeed it encompassed the world. As he saw it, while America is unique in its origins and history, its significance stems from the fact that God's gift is universal and open to all peoples, everywhere.

America has the strength of a free people, which no elite ruling through government or an aristocratic class system could ever match. Indeed, elite claims to authority go against the grain of a free people. As Reagan told a group of Russian students, "Freedom is the recognition that no single person, no single authority or government has a monopoly on the truth, but that every individual life is infinitely precious, that every one of us put on this world has been put there for a reason and has something to offer." On another occasion, he said, "I ask you to trust yourselves. That's what America is all about. Our struggle for nationhood, our unrelenting fight for freedom, our very existence—these have all rested on the assurance that you must be free to shape your life as you are best able to, that no one can stop you from reaching higher or take from you the creativity that has made America the envy of all mankind."

Reagan fought the forces that he viewed as limiting freedom: expanding domestic regulation he regarded as a "silent form of socialism," the totalitarian temptation internationally. His twin goals were to cut back the rapid centralization of government authority in the United States since the 1930s and to confront and challenge—rather than coddle and coexist with—Communism. That part of his vision was constant from the early 1950s on; and while a minority view for a time, it was in no way unique. What was and remains distinctive was his belief in the inevitable triumph of his vision.

Frederick Hayek, author of *The Road to Serfdom* (the 1944 classic attack on socialism), famously dedicated his work to "the socialists of all parties." Hayek conceded, "If it is no longer fashionable to emphasize that 'we are all socialists now,' this is merely because the fact is too obvious. Scarcely anybody doubts that we must continue to move toward socialism."

Scarcely anybody except . . . Ronald Reagan. He exhibited an unswerving belief in the superiority of free societies over those relying on the planning of an elite. He laid out the case for his optimism in an important and prescient speech to the British Parliament in 1982:

> We're approaching the end of a bloody century plagued by a terrible political invention—totalitarianism. Optimism comes less easily today, not because democracy is less vigorous, but because democracy's enemies have refined their instruments of repression. Yet optimism is in order, because day by day democracy is proving itself to be a not-at-all fragile flower. From Stettin on the Baltic to Varna on the Black Sea, the regimes planted by totalitarianism have had more than thirty years to establish their legitimacy. But none—not one regime—has yet to risk free elections. Regimes planted by bayonets do not take root.

The American journalist Lincoln Steffens famously said of his visit to the then-new Bolshevik Russia: "I have seen the future and it works." Reagan countered: "In an ironic sense Karl Marx was right. We are witnessing today a great revolutionary crisis, a crisis where the demands of the economic order are conflicting directly with those of the political order. But the crisis is happening not in the free, non-Marxist West, but in the home of Marxist-Leninism, the Soviet Union. It is the Soviet Union which runs against the tide of history by denying human freedom and human dignity to its citizens."

Reagan closed that speech with a challenge that made explicit the subversive power of freedom viewed as something sought by all peoples, everywhere: "So, let us ask ourselves, 'What kind of people do we think we are?' And let us answer, 'Free people, worthy of freedom and determined not only to remain so but to help others gain their freedom as well.'" He intended that his rhetoric advance a "policy of expansionism" by the democracies to counter the ongoing military expansionism of the Communist states.

Reagan's view of freedom was not synonymous with unbridled materialism, disconnected from moral considerations. As he said to the students of Moscow State University in 1988:

Freedom, it has been said, makes people selfish and materialistic, but Americans are one of the most religious peoples on earth. Because they know that liberty, just as life itself, is not earned but a gift from God, they seek to share that gift with the world. "Reason and experience," said George Washington in his farewell address, "both forbid us to expect that national morality can prevail in exclusion of religious principle. And it is substantially true, that virtue or morality is a necessary spring of popular government."

Reagan made this point over and over throughout his career. He was convinced—and he helped the rest of us see—that, as he had put it some years earlier: "No government at any level and for any price can afford the police necessary to assure our safety and our freedom unless the overwhelming majority of us are guided by an inner personal code of morality."

Peace

Peace is the highest aspiration of the American people. We will negotiate for it, sacrifice for it; we will not surrender for it, now or ever.
—RONALD REAGAN, FIRST INAUGURAL ADDRESS, 1981

My deepest hope was that someday our children and our grandchildren could live in a world free of the constant threat of nuclear war.
—RONALD REAGAN, 1991

Reagan's vision necessarily put peace as the top priority; in the nuclear age there was no alternative. But it was not "peace at any price"—the only practical way to achieve peace would be through unassailable strength that would deter any challengers. Reagan's first exposure to a national audience as a political leader came on October 27, 1964, in a speech later called "A Time for Choosing," or "The Speech." With an eye toward Communist regimes that achieved power by the use of force and then threatened to dragoon others into their monochromatic orbit, he challenged Americans:

We cannot buy our security, our freedom from the threat of the [nuclear] bomb by committing an immorality so great as saying to a billion now in slavery behind the Iron Curtain, "Give up your dreams of freedom because to save our own skin, we are willing to make a deal with your slave masters." Alexander Hamilton said, "A nation which can prefer disgrace to danger is prepared for a master, and deserves one." . . . Every lesson in history tells us that the greater risk lies in appeasement, and this is the specter our well-meaning liberal friends refuse to face . . . that their policy of accommodation is appeasement, and it gives no choice between peace and war, only between fight and surrender. If we can continue to accommodate, continue to back and retreat, eventually we have to face the final demand— the ultimatum.

He continued his support of what Barry Goldwater called "peace through strength" throughout his career, ultimately into the presidency. No one doubted that he would dramatically increase spending on defense, and he did not disappoint. But if Reagan was always clear about the need for an unprecedented buildup of defense, including nuclear weapons, he was equally clear that the goal was not merely the absence of armed conflict, but the eventual abolition of nuclear weapons themselves.

In his second inaugural address, presented in January 1985, Reagan cited "progress in restoring our defense capability," in response to the Soviet Union having undertaken "the greatest military buildup in the history of man." From a position of strength, he felt empowered to negotiate toward his ultimate goal: "We're not just discussing limits on a further increase in nuclear weapons; we seek, instead, to reduce their number. We seek the total elimination one day of nuclear weapons from the face of the Earth."

Reagan viewed the prevailing strategic doctrines of the nuclear age as fundamentally immoral. The notion of war had taken a sinister turn in our century:

As recently as World War I—granted the rules were violated at times—we had a set of rules of warfare in which armies didn't make war against civilians: Soldiers fought soldiers. Then came World War II and Hitler's philosophy of total war, which meant the bombing not only of soldiers but of factories that produced their rifles, and if surrounding communities were also hit, that was to be accepted; then as the war progressed, it became common for the combatants simply to attack civilians as part of military strategy.

By the time the 1980s rolled around, we were placing our entire faith in a weapon whose *fundamental target was the civilian population.*

A nuclear war is aimed at people, no matter how often military men like to say, "No, we only aim to hit other missiles."

Seeing that "Soviet citizens . . . were generally indistinguishable from people I had seen all my life on countless streets in America," Reagan concluded: "It's not people who make war, but governments—and people deserve governments that fight for peace in the nuclear age."

From this vision, Reagan successfully concluded the first agreement in history that would eliminate nuclear weapons. The United States and the U.S.S.R. agreed to specific timetables for destruction of certain weapons enforced by unprecedented on-site monitoring.

THE POWER OF REAGAN'S VISION

Most often it's not how handsomely or eloquently you say something, but the fact that your words mean something.
—RONALD REAGAN

Reagan always understood that the single most important role of a leader is to craft a compelling vision. He took great pains to ensure that he communicated effectively, in substance as well as in presentation.

His vision met the criteria identified earlier: simplicity, flexibility, consistency with values, inclusiveness, constancy, optimism, and personification.

The simplicity is evident in the phrase "family, work, neighborhood, freedom, peace." Reagan constantly sought, throughout his career in elective office, to discipline public debate by returning to questions of vision and values. Taking office as governor of California, Reagan declared: "For many years now, you and I have been . . . told there are no simple answers to the complex questions which are beyond our comprehension. Well, the truth is, there are simple answers—there are just not easy ones." In his memoirs, General Colin Powell (who served as Reagan's national security adviser) offered a quotation he felt captured the essence of Reagan's leadership: "Great leaders are almost always great simplifiers, who cut through argument, debate and doubt, to offer a solution everybody can understand."

The power of simplicity in a vision has been demonstrated repeatedly throughout history. Simplicity ensures that a vision can be remembered by listeners and passed along to others, almost effortlessly. It also makes possible its rapid transmission into implementing management. Of course, such simplicity is often the product of sophistication, disciplined listening, skill, and experience, all tirelessly applied. This will be immediately recognized by those who have composed an organizational mission statement.

Reagan's vision also included great flexibility within its firm principles. Though this may appear paradoxical at first glance, it is not. A powerful vision tends to have an overarching goal, or a principle, as its endpoint. Such a vision not only can have broad reach, but also allows for implementation to be creative and to take various, even unforeseen, directions. It might also include elements that are initially in contradiction or conflict, elements that might or might not ultimately be reconciled, depending on subsequent events. Great enterprises, whether empires or nations or businesses, continue to prosper over time because their visions can encompass such operating flexibility. Among other things, this ensures that they continue to learn.

Perhaps the most notable element adding power to Reagan's vision was its consistency with the values and history of America. Leading the nation out of a time of formless and enervating uncertainty, Reagan consciously evoked old verities to empower people to move forward. In his final address to the nation as president in 1989, he repeated the point he had made so often in the past:

[I] won a nickname, "The Great Communicator." But I never thought it was my style or the words I used that made a difference: It was the content. I wasn't a great communicator, but I communicated great things, and they didn't spring full bloom from my brow, they came from the heart of a great nation— from our experience, our wisdom, and our belief in the principles that have guided us for two centuries. They called it the Reagan Revolution. Well, I'll accept that, but for me it always seemed more like the great rediscovery, a rediscovery of our values and common sense.

Armed with the power of familiar truths from our past, Reagan consciously led America into an era of far greater change and upheaval than that which had precipitated the crisis of confidence he inherited in the early 1980s. While politicians and historians will differ as to the historical significance of Reagan, it is clear that his vision encompassed the unprecedented changes at the end of the 20th century. These include the collapse of the Soviet empire, the defeat of the idea of socialism, the globalization of markets through trade and finance, and the shifting of authority and responsibility from centralized organizations of all types to smaller, more local enterprises and to individuals. In linking these changes with traditional, shared American values and experiences, Reagan's vision provided context and encouragement to people facing the difficulties and potential disorientation of such dizzying change.

The extraordinary inclusiveness of Reagan's vision had at least two notable consequences. It empowered America as a whole, built on a continual infusion of new immigrants, by reminding one and all of their irreplaceable, sacred place in our national family. Internationally, it also had an important place in the context of our ideological struggle with the Soviet Union during the 1980s. In his suggestion that all people shared the potential for American-style freedom, Reagan was urging his potential "customers" across the world to compare the reality of American life with that offered in Communist nations.

No one who has observed Ronald Reagan could fail to be struck by his unshakable optimism. It is important to emphasize that optimism was not only a key part of his presentation of his vision—it was also embedded within his vision. At the time he assumed the presidency his optimism was a distinctive statement that set him apart from his opponents. As he said in his address to the Republican National Convention in 1992: "Well I've said it before and I'll say it again—America's best days are yet to come. Our proudest moments are yet to be. Our most glorious achievements are just ahead. America remains what Emerson called her 150 years ago, "the country of tomorrow."

General Powell has a "rule" he applies to the business of life: "Optimism is a force multiplier." Surely no leader has demonstrated the truth of that approach more effectively than Ronald Reagan. When members of an organization are convinced that tomorrow will be better for them than today, the beneficial effects can range from enhanced morale (as important as that alone can be) to a greater focus on the good of the group over individual desires.

Reagan was faithful to his vision, demonstrating constancy. Ultimately, through a rare combination of decisive action and superior communication skills, he came to personify his vision, propelling it with unmatched force.

———— ◆◆◆ ————

REAGAN ON LEADERSHIP: CRAFT A COMPELLING VISION

- Remember that vision is the indispensable key to leadership of any enterprise.

- Work hard to keep your vision simple, so it can be readily communicated and implemented by others, far beyond your direct efforts.

- Keep your vision at the level of principle and strategy, able to encompass flexibility, creativity, and continuous improvement as it is implemented.

- Ensure that your vision is consistent with the values and history of the members of your organization and your customers. Such consistency becomes increasingly important to the extent that your vision will bring change in its wake or threaten existing arrangements.

- Make your vision as inclusive as possible—bringing out the best in your own organization and tempting others, even competitors, toward your vision.

- Adhere to your vision with unshakable constancy.

- Communicate your vision with infectious optimism; as far as possible incorporate optimism into your vision.

- To the maximum possible extent, personify your vision for your organization.

CHAPTER 2

BE DECISIVE

———————◆◆———————

His most outstanding leadership quality
was that you knew where he stood.
—REAGAN AS DESCRIBED BY
NEWSMAN SAM DONALDSON

When all is said and done the greatest quality required in a
commander is "decision"; he must be able to issue clear orders
and have the drive to get things done. Indecision and hesitation
are fatal in any officer; in a [commander-in-chief] they are criminal.
—FIELD MARSHALL MONTGOMERY OF EL ALAMEIN

A COMPELLING VISION is the foundation of leadership; it is indispensable. Nonetheless it is only the foundation—decisions transform vision into reality.

Virtually everyone has seen firsthand the difference between organizations in which the leadership was decisive and those directed with vacillation. In some families children receive little direction from parents as to right and wrong, leaving the young to fend for themselves in discerning a moral universe. In others the parents leave clear markers, hopefully enforced predictably. While the children may chafe at such demarcation, they at least have the comfort of a degree of certainty and predictability in their daily lives and expectations.

The same traits are seen in business enterprises. Where leadership is viewed as decisive, decisions throughout the chain of command can be made rapidly and with confidence. This makes it possible to seize opportunities or confront dangers in the most opportune manner. One of the advantages small companies and entrepreneurs have in competing with large private or public enterprises is their ability (or necessity!) to make strategic decisions rapidly in a changing environment. A hallmark of great corporations such as Microsoft or Intel is their hard-earned ability to maintain some of the decision-making characteristics of a small company, backed by the resources of an established enterprise.

The decisions that cause a leader to be considered *decisive*—synonymous with the older term *resolute*—have additional characteristics as well. Most important, they directly, understandably, and unavoidably implicate the vision of the organization. Whatever action is taken, or not taken, will have consequences for the core mission of the group.

Such decisions necessarily involve considerable risk. All understand that making the wrong decision—or having the "right" decision fail for reasons outside of one's control or foresight—could have significant consequences. These might range from a missed opportunity (which might be viewed as having scant present effect but major future impact) to an immediate, direct, undeniable, irremediable loss to the organization. Maintaining a strong hand on the tiller in the midst of unavoidable uncertainty arising from incomplete information calls upon the leader's personal resources: conviction, intuition, experience, foresight, knowledge, steadiness, constancy, and courage.

Equally important, these decisions involve unmistakable personal risk to the leader. In some instances, where the leader personifies the organization, this is automatically assumed given the risk to the organization. In others, the liability may be as much or more to the leader himself as to the enterprise. Either way, decisive action under such circumstances reminds others within the organization that everyone, beginning at the top, must place the welfare of the group ahead of personal concerns. The importance of this aspect is perhaps most visible in military organizations.

Decisions of this magnitude must be made at the right time. Outside circumstances may be fluid; one's ability to understand them may decline. One's internal situation, beginning with the morale of the team, may not be as strong with the passage of time—particularly if delay is equated with uncertainty. As General George S. Patton stated: "A good plan violently executed *now* is better than a perfect plan next week."

Critically, when such a decision is made, the leader must stick with it, even if—indeed, especially if—resistance is intense. This becomes a greater factor when the decision affects many people, the uncertainty of result is high, and there is a long time interval between the decision and the result. By his immovability amid the storm, the leader—now personifying the decision—should strive to become the reference point from which all others can navigate.

Decisive action, when the results are successful, greatly strengthens the leader's ongoing ability to direct the enterprise. Where the risks are recognized as great, the results are rapid, and the linkage with the organizational vision is tight, decisive action sets an example that can be repeated by others. It is a vital factor in inspiring trust in the leader; he is aligning his actions with his words under the most difficult of circumstances.

Finally, when a leader is viewed as decisive, changes occur in the broader environment in which the organization operates. Competitors or challengers who may have discounted the significance of the leader's vision, or thought it would not be actualized, must contend with new realities. These realities may extend well beyond the changes wrought by the decision itself. The organization they have encountered may have been transformed by the decisive leadership, occasioning the need to rethink competitive strategy. What is more, their own members may have been demoralized, just as morale soars in their invigorated counterpart. Whatever the specifics, they will have to contend with a changed environment in which another has seized the power of initiative.

Ronald Reagan instinctively understood the importance of decisiveness to leadership. He acted decisively on numerous occasions, ranging from sending troops to the University of California at Berkeley campus (as governor) to committing the nation to a strategic missile defense program. This chapter will focus on three examples that shed light on Reagan's approach.

THE AIR TRAFFIC CONTROLLERS' STRIKE

The strike was an important juncture for our new
administration. I think it convinced people who might
have thought otherwise that I meant what I said.
—RONALD REAGAN

In his first months in the presidency, Reagan faced—and faced down—a challenge that established him as a decisive leader: the strike of the Professional Air Traffic Controllers Organization (PATCO). On August 3, 1981, the union's executive board rejected a proposed agreement, and over 70 percent of the Federal Aviation Administration's 17,000 air traffic controllers went on strike.

The air traffic controllers' strike presented vexing questions. On the one hand, Reagan agreed that a salary increase was justified, despite inflationary implications for the broader economy, because of the "unusual pressures and demands" of the work. On the other hand, PATCO represented government employees, each of whom had signed a sworn affidavit not to strike as a condition of employment. Further complicating matters, PATCO was one of a small number of union organizations that endorsed Republican candidate Reagan against Democrat Carter in the 1980 election. What is more, Reagan himself had a union background: He was the first president who was a lifetime member of the AFL-CIO. He served for six terms as president of the Screen Actors Guild and led its first strike.

The stakes were high. Reagan later recalled: "I suppose this was the first real national emergency I faced as president. The strike endangered the safety of thousands of passengers on hundreds of airline flights daily, and threatened more harm to our already troubled economy." The threshold decision was whether the government would negotiate with a public employee union that was striking illegally.

Reagan viewed the strike as a matter of principle:

No president could tolerate an illegal strike by Federal employees. Unions can strike a business and shut it down, but you cannot allow a strike to shut down a vital government service.

Governments are different from private industry. I agreed with Calvin Coolidge, who said, "There is no right to strike against the public safety by anybody, anywhere, at any time."

Reagan's analysis inexorably led to one conclusion: The strikers were in violation of the law and their own contracts, and must be fired. But the countervailing factors were also strong. Given the expense and time required to train new controllers, there was the possibility that it could be years before

the workforce would return to prestrike levels. In the meantime, there would be understandable public concern about
passenger safety. What is more, as Reagan and his staff surely
recognized, any aviation accident, whatever the cause, might
be linked back—at least in the public mind—to the president's decision. Counsels of compromise were by no means
irrational and indeed might have been the safer route in the
short term.

Nonetheless, Reagan rapidly came to his decision: "I never
had any doubt how to respond to [the strike]." As he later
looked back: "We had the choice of caving in to unreasonable
demands while keeping our air traffic system operating without incident, or of taking a stand for what we thought was
right with the risk of throwing the system into possible chaos.
I felt we had to do what was right."

Reagan spoke to the nation in a televised address from the
White House Rose Garden on the day the strike began. To
make the point at issue plain to the public, he quoted directly
from the sworn affidavit signed by the controllers, uncondi-
tionally committing them not to strike for the duration of
their jobs. Nonetheless, Reagan did not summarily fire those
employees who had been acting illegally since going on strike
at seven o'clock that morning. Instead, he presented an ultimatum that was at once decisive, magnanimous, reasonable—
and shifted the burden of action to the strikers: "It is for this
reason that I must tell those who fail to report for duty this
morning they are in violation of the law, and if they do not
report for work within forty-eight hours, they have forfeited
their jobs and will be terminated."

By acting decisively, Reagan sent a strong signal that his
leadership was to be taken seriously. Acting with dispatch,
clearly comfortable with his own instincts, communicating
his views with skill to the American people, Reagan established that his words were to be heeded. In turning down

a pay increase request that he found unreasonable and inflationary, he also sent a message to management generally. The significance of his action did not go unnoticed abroad. As a prominent American expert on the Soviet Union stated: "The way the PATCO strike was handled impressed the Russians . . . and gave them respect for Reagan. It showed them a man who, when aroused, will go to the limit to back up his principles."

THE GRENADA INTERVENTION

We didn't ask anybody, we just did it.
—RONALD REAGAN

On Friday, October 21, 1983, President and Mrs. Reagan flew to Georgia for a weekend of golf at the Augusta National Golf Course. They were accompanied by Secretary of State George Shultz, new National Security Adviser Bud McFarlane, and other officials. Aware that events were breaking fast in the small but strategically located Caribbean nation of Grenada, Reagan considered postponing the trip. In the end, he concluded that such a last-moment change of plan could trigger speculation by outside observers.

Just after 4:00 A.M. on Saturday, McFarlane placed a telephone call to the president, awakening him to ask for an immediate meeting, along with Shultz. The Organization of Eastern Caribbean States (OECS) had requested that the United States intervene militarily against the apparently emerging Communist government in Grenada. The OECS nations—Antigua and Barbuda, Dominica, Grenada, Montserrat, Saint Lucia, Saint Kitts-Nevis, and Saint Vincent and the Grenadines—were led by Eugenia Charles, prime minister of

Dominica, who had been subject to a coup attempt from Grenada just a year before.

Although the crisis in Grenada had begun during the previous week, the precise timing of the urgent request for American assistance could not have been foreseen. On Wednesday, October 19, nearly a week after being placed under house arrest in a military coup, Prime Minister Maurice Bishop was executed by firing squad. The new government, terming itself a "revolutionary military council," immediately imposed a curfew under martial law. Observers concluded that the new government was trained and backed by the Cuban Communist regime.

The urgency of the threat was heightened—and potential application of U.S. military power was greatly complicated— by the presence of nearly a thousand American students attending medical school. In a time when hostage taking and terrorism were commonplace, the implications were plain.

To protect American options, during the previous week Reagan had ordered naval ships rerouted toward Grenada. He had also ordered the Pentagon to draw up plans for a rescue mission.

By the predawn hours on Saturday, events were in the saddle. As Shultz later recounted, the combination of the threat to American lives and the request from Mrs. Charles was irresistible: "President Reagan's reaction was decisive." He ordered that a rescue mission be prepared for execution early the following week. Siding with Shultz and others advocating immediate action, Reagan overrode Defense Secretary Weinberger and another faction that sought delay either to obtain more information or to create a coalition with at least one other country.

A key issue was Reagan's determination that the entire operation be undertaken in secrecy. He did not want to provide forewarning that would allow Cuban troops (who could be reinforced rapidly given the short distance separating Grenada and Cuba) or hostile Grenadians to take the students as hostages. To minimize the chance of a press leak, Reagan also decided not to provide advance notice to the government of Margaret Thatcher. He did this in full knowledge of the strain this would place on a valued national alliance and personal friendship; Grenada had been a British colony for nearly 200 years until 1974.

Reagan was also concerned that if he provided a chance for Congress to have input on a military operation under these circumstances, the use of force would not be possible:

> Frankly, there was another reason I wanted secrecy. It was what I call the "post-Vietnam syndrome," the resistance of many in Congress to the use of military force abroad for any reason, because of our nation's experience in Vietnam. . . . I believed the United States couldn't remain spooked forever by this experience to the point where it refused to stand up and defend its legitimate national security interests. I suspected that, if we told the leaders of Congress about the operation, even under terms of strictest confidentiality, there would be some who would leak it to the press together with the prediction that Grenada was going to become "another Vietnam."

This approach predictably infuriated many members of Congress and ensured the President's sole accountability for the success or failure of the mission.

The American invasion—which the administration generally referred to as an "intervention" or "rescue mission"—began on Monday evening, October 24. The pressure Reagan doubtless felt was increased dramatically by the ongoing news from Beirut following a horrendous weekend bombing against the American peacekeeping force; by late Monday it was determined that the suicide bomber who detonated 2,000 pounds of TNT had killed 241 marines as they slept.

As the American forces approached the beginning of operations on Monday evening, Reagan invited congressional leaders to the White House to provide them with advance notice of the attack. He met with them at about eight o'clock; the invasion was planned for nine o'clock. While the Republicans supported Reagan, the Democrats were, in Shultz's word, "cool," with Speaker Tip O'Neill particularly sensitive to being informed rather than consulted.

During this meeting, Reagan was called out to accept a call from a "very angry" Margaret Thatcher. Because of Grenada's membership in the British Commonwealth, she demanded that the United States cancel its military operation. Under the circumstances, Reagan felt he could not tell her that it was already under way.

Against this background, it was a profound relief all around when the island was pacified by U.S. forces the next day. Reagan later admitted that even he, already renowned for his unflappable mien, had anxious moments on that Monday evening: "Militarily, we can look back on the operation as a textbook success. When it was going on, though, there were many uncertainties and potential problems, especially regarding the safety of our students; I suspect that none of us who participated in planning the operation slept well the night before."

Even with the success of the operation, there remained significant uncertainty as to how it would be received. Press coverage was at best mixed. Doubtless this reflected, at least in part, a Pentagon decision to limit press access to the operation itself. Congressional reaction was predictably wary, particularly in the context of the simultaneous crisis unfolding in Beirut. Some even called for presidential impeachment and other unlikely remedies. British and European reaction continued to be negative.

By Thursday, October 27, the tide turned. American students disembarking from air force planes gave relieved thanks for their safe return; some even kissed the ground of their native land. Later that day, Reagan's presentation of the case for the Grenada mission, combined with an explanation of the Beirut situation, additionally strengthened public support.

In his memoirs Shultz offered a view of the significance of the Grenada action, quoting from George Will's approving *Newsweek* column of November 7, 1983:

> Grenada, although small, is 15 times the size of Iwo Jima and of large symbolic value. U.S. soldiers' boot prints on Grenada's soil have done more than the MX will do to make U.S. power credible and peace secure. President Reagan's defense budgets are not, by themselves, a fully effective signal to the Soviet Union of U.S. seriousness. The boot prints prove that the United States will not only procure sophisticated weapons systems but also has recovered the will to use the weapon on which its security rests: the man with a rifle.

RESPONDING TO QADDAFI

I felt we couldn't ignore the mad clown of Tripoli any longer.
—RONALD REAGAN

Another example of Reagan's decisiveness—one that involved methodical escalation over time—involved the Libyan despot, Colonel Muammar Qaddafi. Qaddafi was linked to the use of terror across the world, including inside the United States. Intelligence reports indicated that the Soviet Union was exporting arms to his regime, which in turn gave succor and support to affiliated organizations across the world.

In May 1981, following an FBI investigation linking a Libyan terrorist to a murder in Chicago, the Reagan administration ordered the closure of the Libyan embassy in Washington. In June Reagan was presented with the decision of whether to authorize the Sixth Fleet to conduct maneuvers in the Gulf of Sidra. The Carter administration had discontinued annual maneuvers in the previous year as part of its Iranian hostage negotiations. As a signal to Qaddafi, as well as to other nations that might use Qaddafi's action as a precedent to limit American access to international waters adjacent to their shores, Reagan ordered them to go forward.

Shortly before the Gulf of Sidra maneuvers were to begin in August, an admiral sought clarification on the "rules of engagement" for American forces. The Libyans were already harassing American ships and aircraft in the region, and in all likelihood would accelerate their activities as a response to the maneuvers.

Reagan answered by defining the issue as a matter of principle: "Any time we send an American anywhere in the world where he or she can be shot at, they have the right to shoot back."

The admiral then wished to know the extent to which American planes could pursue Libyan planes that were engaging in such harassment.

As Reagan told it:

> The admiral stopped, cleared his throat, and looked over at me, waiting for an answer from me, and suddenly it was very quiet in the room.
>
> "All the way into the hangar," I said.
>
> A smile broke out on the admiral's face, and he said, "Yes, sir."

A few international leaders supported Reagan's strong stance vis-à-vis Qaddafi—most notably Anwar Sadat of Egypt, who would soon die in a hail of assassins' bullets that many believed were traceable to Qaddafi. Others were queasy.

Some European leaders, representing nations close to Libya, perceived themselves as especially vulnerable to terror and were simultaneously desirous of expanded trade.

Terrorist acts linked to Libya, or at least encouraged and applauded by Libya's regime, continued. In December 1985 Palestinian terrorists indiscriminately fired automatic weapons into holiday crowds at Rome and Vienna airports, killing 20 people, including 5 Americans. Qaddafi praised the attack as a "noble act"; investigators concluded that at least one terrorist had demonstrably been assisted by the Libyan government.

Reagan was prepared to act. Although the president had "a full shelf of contingency plans designed to express in a concrete way our displeasure with [Libyan] terrorism," he was constrained by the presence of nearly a thousand American oil field workers there. There was little question that they could be made hostages in the event of military retaliation by the United States.

In March 1986 the American Sixth Fleet undertook additional maneuvers in the Gulf of Sidra. The U.S. ships were directed to ignore Qaddafi's self-proclaimed "line of death," the boundary he drew more than a hundred miles off the Libyan coast, far beyond the customary 12-mile limit recognized across the world. Again, Reagan ordered the American forces to respond if attacked.

Two days into the maneuvers, the Libyans fired surface-to-air missiles at American planes and sent offensive ships within firing range of the American fleet. With Reagan's approval, the U.S. forces sank the Libyan ships and immobilized radar facilities used for Libyan missile attacks.

On April 5, the Libyan gangster responded. In a wanton act of terror, a bomb was detonated in a disco in West Berlin favored by American troops. In addition to claiming the lives of an American soldier and a Turkish woman, the bomb injured more than 200 people, including at least 50 American servicemen.

Qaddafi disregarded his past practice of publicly praising the application of terror against the United States. Perhaps reflecting concern about the recent American military actions, he instead condemned the Berlin bombing, implying that he was just another bystander. However, on the basis of American intelligence reports, Reagan became convinced that "the evidence was irrefutable" that "Libya was responsible for the bombing."

With the American oil field workers now out of Libya, a key deterrent to American retaliation had been removed, but a problem remained: how to avoid harm to innocent people during a retaliatory attack. Since the point of retaliation was to punish Qaddafi for his sponsorship of the use of terror against innocents, this was no small point.

On April 14 the United States retaliated against Tripoli and Benghazi, reportedly unleashing nearly a hundred 2,000-pound bombs. As feared, numerous Libyan civilians—probably more than a hundred—lost their lives. The principal target, which Reagan understood to be "located well away from civilian targets," was Qaddafi's military headquarters and barracks in Tripoli. This facility allegedly housed the intelligence center directing the Libyan terrorist network.

Reagan publicly maintained that there was no intention to murder Qaddafi himself in the raid. This was in conformance with American law banning the use of political assassination as a policy tool. However, several bombs hit the area of the dictator's living quarters, killing Qaddafi's adopted daughter and wounding two of his sons. Off-the-record comments by administration officials at the time did not convey sufficient shock or disappointment to overcome widespread suspicion about the intent of those bombs.

In a televised address to the nation on April 14, 1986,

Reagan announced the military action. After recapitulating the history of Qaddafi's use of terror, he presented a principle that was clear and consistent with his vision: "When our citizens are abused or attacked anywhere in the world on the direct orders of a hostile regime, we will respond so long as I'm in this Oval Office. Self-defense is not only our right, it is our duty. It is the purpose behind the mission undertaken tonight, a mission fully consistent with Article 51 of the United Nations Charter."

Later in the same address, Reagan reminded the American people—as well as listeners worldwide—that the United States was in no way acting precipitately: "We Americans are slow to anger. We always seek peaceful avenues before resorting to the use of force—and we did. We tried quiet diplomacy, public condemnation, economic sanctions, and demonstrations of military force. None succeeded. Despite our repeated warnings, Qaddafi continued his reckless policy of intimidation, his relentless pursuit of terror. He counted on America to be passive. He counted wrong."

America, in Reagan's presentation, was not only walking tall—it was prepared to walk alone if necessary. Even if the entire town was paralyzed by cowardice, America was willing to take to the street alone, like Gary Cooper's sheriff in the classic *High Noon,* if that was the only way to deal with armed and dangerous criminals: "I warned that there should be no place on earth where terrorists can rest and train and practice their deadly skills. I meant it. I said that we would act with others, if possible, and alone if necessary to ensure that terrorists have no sanctuary anywhere. Tonight, we have."

In the event the United States had acted largely alone. Press reports of imminent American military action had sparked broad denunciation across Europe and the Third World. France and Italy even declined to allow the United States to fly across their air space for purposes of attack.

In the United States the president acted—once again—prior to consulting the congressional leadership. Instead he merely informed them of the impending attack as it was about to begin, precluding them from expressing public or private opposition prospectively. As with the Grenada case earlier, this led to anger and immediate criticism by the political opposition and greatly increased the risk that the mission placed directly on Reagan.

To appreciate the decisive approach taken by Reagan, one must remember the magnitude of the risk and uncertainty he faced. As Reagan stressed in his April 14 speech, he had "no illusion that tonight's action will ring down the curtain on Qaddafi's reign of terror." In fact at least one American and two Britons were murdered on the orders of Qaddafi in retaliation for the raid. There was also no guarantee that Qaddafi and his allies would not choose to escalate their use of terror, perhaps bringing it home to the United States. As it turned out, some additional Libyan terror against Americans may have occurred, though it appeared to have declined dramatically and certainly was not publicly flaunted as in the past.

There was also considerable risk to various international priorities. In the always volatile Middle East, the public reactions of leaders were generally negative, and there was additional concern for the well-being of American hostages already held in the region. The division vis-à-vis the European alliance was disconcerting, particularly in the context of ongoing military balance negotiations between the NATO powers and the Soviet Union. For its part, the U.S.S.R., doubtless with an eye not only toward Europe but also to the Middle East and the Third World nations generally, officially deplored the American military action. Not only did they have their spokesman describe Qaddafi as a victim of aggression, but they also canceled a high-level meeting in preparation for a U.S.–U.S.S.R. summit.

Of course, all these risks would be magnified if the initial mission itself were viewed as a failure in military terms. Given the logistical issues, particularly those imposed by the French and Italian governments—whose intransigence over use of their air space caused some American planes to fly more than a thousand additional miles en route to their targets—this was no small consideration. A strike that was successful in military terms might nonetheless have been viewed by Western publics as a failure or a ghastly and disproportionate use of force if the cost in terms of innocent lives was perceived to be too high. Even Margaret Thatcher, the resolute and unsentimental "Iron Lady," expressed concern to Reagan prior to the air strike about the potential for civilian losses.

However, Reagan's decision paid off. He had sent yet another signal of his strength in adhering to his principles. Many recognized—doubtless including some who publicly opposed the military action—that he had laid the groundwork justifying the use of force methodically over an extended period. It was difficult to credibly portray him as a warmonger or as trigger-happy. At home most Americans who were polled expressed support for his action, while foreign leaders were reminded yet again of his unusual willingness to take decisive action—standing virtually alone if necessary—to back up his words.

THE IMPORTANCE OF DECISIVENESS

What Sam Donaldson said about Reagan is what people tend to say about decisive leaders: You know where they stand. As a result, you also know where *you* stand. This is true whether you are part of the same organization, a competitor, or an observer. Decisiveness, when it reflects the vision of the leader, encourages trust in the leader. Where a decision entails a great amount of risk, perhaps requiring courage, constancy, and perseverance in the face of challenge or uncertainty, the degree of trust engendered by a satisfactory outcome is heightened.

In some cases, the trust and resulting sense of certainty earned by decisiveness can override an observer's disagreement with the underlying action. It is a truism that many people voted for and supported Ronald Reagan even though they disagreed with his stance on one or more issues of importance to them. Some people seemed to respect him all the more for his strongly held views in the face of disagreement and criticism. To be sure he was predictable in not trimming his sails on unpopular issues such as aid to the Nicaraguan "Contras" or his opposition to legalized abortion.

Most notably, he held firm for his economic program in the midst of the 1981–82 recession, while his approval rating sank to perilously low levels. When the skies brightened, the president who stubbornly urged us to "stay the course" looked strong indeed. As Bennis and Nanus put it, "While his actions were arguably 'the right thing,' Reagan understood that it's not necessarily the direction (the angle you take) that counts, but sticking reasonably to the direction you choose."

As he took decisive action, Reagan took pains to present the context to the public and to make clear the connection with his broader vision. In the case of Grenada, for example, public support markedly increased following his address to the nation.

The reservoir of trust and respect gained from decisive action well-communicated can serve the leader well when circumstances dictate a detour, real or apparent, from his vision. For example, Governor Reagan's unflinching advocacy of the death penalty left few to question his decision to grant clemency to a convicted murderer who was brain damaged. Had someone tried to argue that Reagan's position on the death penalty was unclear or compromised by this decision, he would have lacked credibility. Some observers felt that Bill

Clinton's decision, as a presidential candidate, to fly home to Arkansas to ensure the execution of an allegedly brain-damaged killer was necessitated by the absence of that kind of credibility for his own avowed support of the death penalty.

Similarly, public confidence in Reagan's toughness vis-à-vis the Soviet Union enabled him to overlook provocations that could have derailed or at least delayed progress toward nuclear arms reduction agreements. An example was the so-called Daniloff affair, in which the Soviets alleged, without foundation, that an American journalist was a spy. Nonetheless, Reagan was able to preserve American public support for moving ahead with a scheduled summit conference with his Russian counterpart. A leader with less credibility might have felt he had no alternative but to take disproportionate action arguably against the nation's higher interest.

It is important to remember that, in the end, whether a leader is considered "decisive" depends on the successful denouement of his decisions. Presumably the leader of the PATCO union, Robert E. Poli, believed he was taking decisive action in calling the 1981 strike. In a sense, he was—but he lost the fight and his leadership position as well.

REAGAN ON LEADERSHIP: BE DECISIVE

- Recognize that a willingness to take decisive action is a hallmark of an effective leader—people want to know where you stand so they will know where they stand.

- Decisive action must be taken in a timely manner—an action taken too late, even if executed with greater precision, may have much less value.

- Decisive actions that put the leader at visible risk set an example that strengthens the organization.

- By aligning work and deeds, decisive actions add predictability and certainty to an enterprise.

- A leader should make plain, both before and after decisive actions are taken, how their accomplishment relates to the vision of the organization.

- In cases where immediate action is not an option, be prepared to take a methodical approach, laying markers that will make eventual action comprehensible and defensible.

- Be willing to take sole accountability for a decisive action that goes to the core of your vision—if necessary, act alone.

- The trust earned from taking decisive actions may provide the leader with the benefit of the doubt when circumstances force him to take actions that are, or might be made to appear, inconsistent with his vision.

- While taking decisive action may bring to bear many positive characteristics of the leader, none of that will matter if the action is not a success.

CHAPTER 3

NEGOTIATE
FROM STRENGTH

Before I took up my current line of work, I got to know
a thing or two about negotiating when I represented the
Screen Actors Guild in contract talks with the studios.
After the studios, Gorbachev was a snap.
—RONALD REAGAN

ONE OF THE most important skills, required of virtually everyone, is the ability to negotiate effectively. Perhaps
the family is the cradle of negotiation experience. With constantly changing circumstances imposed by births, deaths,
marriages, illness, growth, and the aging process, family members constantly renegotiate their relationships.

Negotiation is a key to every business relationship; indeed
the English word *negotiate* is derived from the Latin "to trans-
act business." Every transaction involves coming to agreement
to achieve a specific result. This ranges from getting a loan
from the bank to coming to terms on an employment contract.

Some people assume that as leaders rise to high levels in
organizations, their need to negotiate declines. Presumably,
such leaders can rely on their ability to give orders. Perhaps

that view would accurately depict the theory of the military chain of command. In the armed forces, strict hierarchies are established, based on the assurance that orders given from above will be executed without hesitation or question, much less dissent. Yet even in the military such a view is incomplete. Many of the greatest commanders have been superb negotiators—and they had to be. Dwight Eisenhower, for example, as the supreme Allied commander in the Second World War, exhibited extraordinary negotiating skills working with other Allied leaders, as well as with the president and the Congress at home.

In most enterprises, the necessity for negotiating skills increases rather than decreases as one earns greater authority. This is especially clear in the case of the American presidency. It is a commonplace that the presidency is the most powerful office in the world. In many ways it may well be the most powerful office—at least from the outside looking in. Presidents quickly learn, however, that there are many centers of authority and power with which they must negotiate.

The leading presidential scholar of our time, Richard E. Neustadt, cites the warnings of outgoing President Harry Truman as he considered the challenges that General Eisenhower would face should he become—as of course he did become—President Eisenhower: "He'll sit here," Truman would remark (tapping his desk for emphasis), "and he'll say, 'Do this! Do that!' *And nothing will happen.* Poor Ike—it won't be a bit like the Army. He'll find it very frustrating." As Truman had earlier said, "I sit here all day trying to persuade people to do the things they ought to have sense enough to do without my persuading them. . . . That's all the powers of the President amount to." Whether dealing with foreign nations, governors, lobbying groups, members of Congress, or sometimes even with the executive bureaucracies they head, commanders-in-chief must also be negotiators-in-chief.

Most people who have held leadership roles, including management roles, will recognize their own experience in Truman's words. Even where one's formal authority is strong—perhaps *especially* where one's formal authority is strong—the need to persuade, to negotiate is great. Often the leader of a large enterprise must negotiate with outside organizations to establish a strategic position or goal and then must bargain within his own organization to ensure implementation. The internal negotiation, by whatever name or process, may be both necessary and difficult, even though formal authority clearly rests with the leader.

Many presidents come into office with significant experience in negotiation. As the top general of the American Revolution, George Washington brought extraordinary leadership skills of all types, including negotiating skills. Abraham Lincoln brought the skills of a wily, analytical, flexible—at times cunning—lawyer. Theodore and Franklin Roosevelt each combined the executive experience of having been governor of what was then the nation's most populous and important state with prior service in the federal executive branch. Lyndon Johnson, having served as the U.S. Senate majority leader, possessed highly developed negotiating skills, particularly in legislative-executive relations. Richard Nixon, having served as an understudy of sorts to President Eisenhower, and as a student of history and leadership, had a distinct approach to negotiation as well.

Nonetheless, it is unlikely that any president had so fully considered the role of negotiation—and the negotiator—as Ronald Reagan. Like other individuals who begin their lives making their own way, without family or other resources to fall back on, Reagan early on had to learn to fend for himself. In his case this included the need to negotiate employment agreements with several radio stations, and then with Hollywood studios. His leadership skills were recognized by his

peers, who elected him to six terms as the president of the
Screen Actors Guild. This was a tough, high-stakes business.
Reagan proudly recalled, "I'd matched wits with some of the
shrewdest negotiators on the planet—people like Jack Warner,
Y. Frank Freeman, the president of Paramount, MGM's Louis
B. Mayer, and the heads of the other studios." Later, as a suc-
cessful governor of California, he acquired additional negoti-
ating skills.

LAYING THE GROUNDWORK
FOR NEGOTIATION

Reagan's negotiation technique followed a set pattern. The
first step was preparation. He described this step in an interview prior to the Reykjavik summit with Gorbachev in 1986:
"It's the initial phase of the negotiating process laying the
groundwork, setting the agenda, establishing areas of agreement as well as disagreement that pays off in the future." He
added: "Now, if that's true of labor and management negotiations here, you can imagine how relevant it is to Soviet-
American bargaining sessions; after all, we have a little more
separating us than, say, General Motors and the UAW."

To lay the groundwork, Reagan would use his communication skills, making points publicly. In some cases that meant
direct pressure on the adversary and his negotiating position.
For example, in 1971, beginning his second term as governor,
his top priority was welfare reform. The legislative leadership
was so hostile that it denied Reagan's request for a joint session to present his proposals. Rather than retreat, Reagan
sensed an opportunity. He campaigned across the state, giving the speech "they wouldn't let me deliver to the legislature."
The ensuing public support was made manifest to recalcitrant
legislators by an avalanche of cards and letters; serious nego-

tiations began shortly thereafter. Reagan had been able to frame the debate, demonstrate an atmosphere of public support, and seize the initiative through rapid, decisive action. He could now negotiate from a position of strength.

As president, Reagan followed the same approach in laying the groundwork for negotiating with the Congress. On vexing issues such as budgetary priorities and major tax reform he would use the power of his communication skill and rapport with the American people—or the threat of it—to maneuver Congress toward his negotiating stance.

He followed a similar approach, writ large, in dealing with the Soviet Union. When he entered the White House in 1981, he sought to renegotiate the basic, unwritten understandings between the two superpowers. In turn that would be the prelude to the most important negotiation of the era: to reduce and destroy nuclear weaponry as the first step toward ridding the world of nuclear weapons.

Given the breadth of the goal, the groundwork Reagan laid for negotiation was wide-ranging. He altered the public dialogue, publicly describing the Soviet Union in judgmental terms, most notably as the "Evil Empire." He publicly took up the cause of peoples seeking freedom from Soviet tyranny, such as the valiant Poles of the Solidarity union movement. He took decisive action, as in the cases of the illegal PATCO strike and Grenada, that altered expectations—in the U.S.S.R. as elsewhere—about American resolve. He remained steadfast against a background of huge public demonstrations and consequent queasiness of politicians in America and Europe, in guaranteeing the strength of the NATO forces facing the Warsaw Pact in Europe. He exhibited an invincible insouciance toward those in polite circles, including many mainstream commentators here and abroad, who questioned not only his approach to the Soviets, but also his judgment, intelligence, and competence. As Soviet leaders came and went without a

leader-to-leader summit, though he faced a reelection campaign without the thawing in American-Russian relations that
many craved, Reagan worked on his own schedule, convinced
that he should not enter negotiations in the "supplicant" role.

Finally, by late 1983, Reagan was satisfied that the groundwork had been laid. He had come to this conclusion even as
Soviet negotiators had walked out of major negotiations then
in progress. Reagan later described the situation: "The United
States was in its strongest position in two decades to negotiate with the Russians from strength. The American economy
was booming. . . . In spirit and military strength, America was
back, and I figured it would be only a matter of time before the
Soviets were back at the table."

THE PROCESS OF NEGOTIATION

Reagan also had decided opinions about how to enter into
negotiations as the preliminaries moved toward formal meetings: "I don't take too seriously the statement of positions in
advance of negotiations. Everyone wants to preserve their
position at their highest price before negotiations. And for
them to do otherwise is to give away something they might
have to give away once the negotiations start."

Understanding that "you're unlikely to ever get *all* you
want," the positions actually taken in negotiation should allow
for compromise. As Martin Anderson said: "He always asked
for much more than he was either expecting to get or willing
to accept. This was never acknowledged, perhaps even to himself." Reagan practiced this not only by seeking more on a
specific item—say a tax cut—from his opponents, but also by
including additional agenda items. For example, he repeatedly
vexed the Soviets in nuclear arms control talks by also bring-

ing up issues ranging from their invasion of Afghanistan to the plight of their citizens who sought to emigrate to their failure to honor commitments to buy American grain.

While the position offered should be clear and easily explainable, both to the other side and to any relevant outside audiences, there must be no signal of the "bottom line" you believe may be ultimately acceptable. Reagan explained his initial approach to the Intermediate Range Nuclear Forces (INF) negotiations:

> I'd learned as a union negotiator that it's never smart to show your hole card in advance. If we first announced that our goal was the total elimination of intermediate-range nuclear weapons from Europe and then hinted we might be willing to leave a few, we'd be tipping off the bottom line of our negotiating position before the negotiations even began. I thought our goal should be the total elimination of all INF weapons from Europe, and stating this before the world would be a vivid gesture demonstrating to the Soviets, our allies, the people storming the streets of West Germany, and others that we meant business about wanting to reduce nuclear weapons.

As the other side presents its position, it is critical that undivided attention be paid, to understand their offer and its intent. As then-governor Reagan told Lou Cannon, "It pays to listen to what they are offering." Once both sides' positions have been presented, every effort must be made to encourage the other side to come forward first with concessions and to avoid being placed in the position of bidding against oneself. The other side may not only offer more than you anticipate; it may suggest an unforeseen alternative that is preferable to your own offer or perhaps even your own bottom line. Of course, one's ability to accomplish this depends upon the groundwork laid, the time available, and the skill of the individuals in the negotiation.

While one must be tough in negotiation, care should be taken not to turn adversaries into enemies. Reagan cautioned: "You'll probably get more of what you want if you don't issue ultimatums and leave your adversary room to maneuver; you shouldn't back your adversary into a corner, embarrass him, or humiliate him." Fellow actor Charlton Heston has described this aspect of Reagan's negotiating style, as applied during the first strike of the Screen Actors Guild: "He was always good-humored. He would never take a confrontational position; he was not dogmatic. He might disagree, but he'd find a way to leave the other side with a feeling that they were good guys, too, and not the enemy. That is hard to do in such situations."

He hewed carefully to this approach, which can expand the possibilities for agreement by increasing trust. It also helped keep issues of ego to a minimum. Gingerly coaxing Ferdinand Marcos off the tiger he had ridden unmercifully as the strong man of the Philippines, Reagan took pains to ensure that Marcos' pride was not unnecessarily bruised. Even in the case of the Soviets—especially in the case of the Soviets—Reagan carefully combined strong bargaining positions with a personal approach to Gorbachev.

The importance of not allowing one's ego to become caught up in the give-and-take of negotiation is closely related to another rule Reagan applied in the most challenging circumstances: Always be prepared to walk away. If discussions have become fruitless, such as when your opposite number continues to try to seek your compromise on an issue previously declared nonnegotiable, you should be prepared to walk out. This is exactly what Reagan did at the celebrated Reykjavik Summit with Gorbachev in October 1986.

As Reagan later summarized: "At Reykjavik, my hopes for a nuclear-free world soared briefly, then fell during one of the longest, most disappointing—and ultimately angriest—days of my presidency." On the final day, as the summit continued past its noon deadline toward the evening, Reagan and Gorbachev were apparently on the brink of a historic breakthrough encompassing elimination of nuclear weapons in Europe as well as all Soviet and American ballistic missiles. Suddenly Gorbachev raised an issue that Reagan had repeatedly declared nonnegotiable: the research and deployment of the American ballistic missile defense program called the Strategic Defense Initiative. Concluding that Gorbachev's demand was a premeditated negotiating ploy that verged on bad faith, a visibly angry Reagan led a walkout by the American delegation.

Kenneth Adelman, a member of Reagan's negotiating team, has described the scene:

> By God that Sunday afternoon in Reykjavik—with the wind howling outside the lofty house and the lofty house supposedly being spooked or haunted as the legend has it in Iceland—and Mikhail Gorbachev and seven thousand reporters outside saying in essence that Ronald Reagan could get the Nobel Prize. He could be a hero if only he would gut SDI—the Strategic Defense Initiative—his own program to protect America. And Mikhail Gorbachev banging away at him like crazy, Ronald Reagan just said no. He wasn't about to pander to those guys outside, the seven thousand press guys, or to Mikhail Gorbachev's blandishments and he just wanted a good arms control agreement but was not willing to settle for any. . . . So it was kind of a magical moment. It was an impressive moment. I don't know many people in my life who would have performed so well at that moment.

The pressure on Reagan was heightened further by the imminent midterm elections at home, just over a week away. All present were also aware that Reagan was in the middle of his final term, moving ineluctably toward lame duck status.

A president preoccupied with his own ego needs, such as speculation about his place in history, might have felt even more stress.

Another issue facing negotiators serving in representative capacities (as in high-level government or labor-management negotiations) is how to respond to outside questions. It is important that any public statement be carefully crafted for its effect on the outside audience as well as those sitting across the table. To do otherwise is to invite an uncontrollable and unpredictable set of forces into your negotiation. Comments on the course of the negotiations themselves, or on tactics or approach, should be scrupulously avoided. As Reagan said during negotiations with Panamanian strongman Manuel Noriega in 1988: "When you're negotiating . . . , you don't go out and talk about what you're negotiating."

As governor and president, Reagan would often delegate the details of negotiations to aides. He would have previously set out the goals of the negotiations, and in some cases reviewed tactical options. While we will discuss Reagan's practices of delegation later, the advantages of this approach to negotiation are worth noting here. It maintains the options for the leader as ultimate decision maker. He can shape responses to the other side based on his views without the combination of unambiguous finality and potential for additional, unintended signals that his direct participation could occasion. For example, Reagan famously told one arms negotiator to inform his Soviet counterpart, who was expected to find an American INF proposal unacceptable: "You just tell the Soviets that you're working for one tough son of a bitch." Given Reagan's unsurpassed experience as a negotiator, delegation preserved his ability to continue to think about negotiating options without the distraction of participating in the actual discussions.

Nonetheless, it may become advantageous for the leader to personally participate in the negotiation. As Reagan observed,

"Sometimes the easiest way to get some things done is for the top people to do them alone and in private." For example, the principals may choose to meet if one or both foresee that the prospective agreement will be a hard sell to those he represents, and the personal word of the other lead negotiator with respect to implementation could be determinative. Similarly, if the stakes are extremely high, or if the terms of the agreement have come close to one or both parties' bottom line, the principals' direct participation may be called for. The principals may also wish to personally negotiate issues that are significant but are best handled in a more intimate way than those on which the public is most focused. An example would be the "quiet diplomacy" Reagan pursued for specific groups seeking human rights in the U.S.S.R. during arms control negotiations.

Sometimes, those at the top are best positioned to bring contentious issues to closure. Facing the bureaucratic pressures against new conceptions being introduced into negotiations, Reagan "felt that if you got the two top people negotiating and talking at a summit and then the two of you came out arm in arm saying, 'We've agreed to this,' the bureaucrats wouldn't be able to louse up the agreement." Leaders of large private organizations face the same issue, albeit on a lesser scale, in dealing with their own corporate bureaucracies.

THE NEGOTIATOR AS LEADER

As important as the *process* of negotiation is, its value can only by judged with reference to the bottom-line *result*. Reagan's approach, which assumes that one is going to get less than one asks for, makes compromise inevitable. Some critics, particularly those who may have supported his initial proposal, could feel betrayed as a result. After leaving public life, Reagan discussed his approach:

> When I began entering into the give and take of legislative bargaining in Sacramento, a lot of the most radical conservatives who had supported me during the election didn't like it. "Compromise" was a dirty word to them and they wouldn't face the fact that we couldn't get all of what we wanted today. They wanted all or nothing and they wanted it all at once.
>
> I'd learned while negotiating union contracts that you seldom got everything you asked for. And I agreed with FDR, who said in 1933: "I have no expectations of making a hit every time I come to the bat. What I seek is the highest possible batting average."

Reagan, like Franklin Roosevelt, believed that history and events were moving in his direction, where some of his supporters assumed it was moving against their goals. It was this optimism that could allow Reagan to conclude, "If you got seventy-five or eighty percent of what you were asking for, I say, you take it and fight for the rest later, and that's what I told these radical conservatives who never got used to it." What some of the critics may not have recognized was that his optimism not only made compromise possible and defensible, but it also provided him with a durable patience that allowed him to extend or even withdraw from negotiations when necessary to achieve his purposes.

Reagan's success as a negotiator was the result of his technique, but the technique was built around his vision and decisiveness. He worked hard to define the terms of the negotiation along the lines of his vision. This was made easier by the fact that his vision was easily translated into broad operating principles: lower taxes, cut regulation, increase defense spending, and so forth. This provided a context both for his own negotiating stance and for the public's understanding of the eventual agreement. Such a context could also strengthen the basis for his optimism for continued future movement in his direction.

Reagan understood that one of the most critical parts of the process occurs after the actual negotiation is complete: the presentation of the agreement to those he represented. As one observer in California wrote: "He would boldly announce a controversial program, quietly modify it in the face of criticism and then hail the compromise as a complete victory." This description, while not inaccurate, does not fully capture the fact that Reagan's focus on presenting the agreement as consistent with his vision kept a discipline on his negotiating positions. His creativity or desire to compromise had to work in tandem with his thoughts of how he might present the agreement to the public. He wanted to be certain that whatever direction he took—on budgets in Sacramento or Washington, or in arms control negotiations with the Soviets— could be credibly presented as consistent with his vision. In that way he would maintain public trust and build momentum toward his long-term goals.

It is instructive to compare Reagan's approach with that of his presidential successors, George Bush and Bill Clinton. Whatever their other merits, Bush and Clinton each failed to present a compelling vision that provided a context for their own negotiations with a Congress controlled by the opposition party. As a result, the agreements resulting from their negotiations on major legislative issues—tax cuts, budget, welfare reform—largely reflected their adversaries' goals. Despite those presidents' efforts to present the results in a different light—even with the incomparable advantage of the presidential "bully pulpit" poised against the cacophony of voices of the Congress—the public generally seemed to understand how much the opposition had really gained.

In the aftermath of a negotiation, Reagan would maintain his discipline in not discussing the tactics he had employed. Even though such talk could no longer harm the completed negotiation, it could obviously have deleterious consequences for future negotiations, either by humiliating his opponents or by limiting Reagan's future application of specific approaches. The silence may also have been magnanimity in victory arising from Reagan's characteristic humility. Martin Anderson has written: "After long and arduous negotiations, his opponent would finally make an offer that was actually far more than Reagan's minimum. Reagan would accept it quickly and quietly, never once boasting how he put one over on the other fellow, but self-content in the knowledge that, once again, he had achieved a substantial victory."

Another practical reason why Reagan would not have discussed his negotiating tactics was that his negotiations never really seemed to end. For example, as he and Gorbachev walked together after the successful conclusion of the INF treaty, planning for future arms reductions, Reagan used the time alone to ask that the Soviets stop shipping military supplies into Nicaragua. Gorbachev agreed.

Reagan, acting as negotiator-in-chief, handled some of the most important issues of his presidency essentially as negotiations. This is most clearly seen in his handling of economic and budgetary confrontations with Congress and arms control parleys with the Soviet Union. An astute observer, journalist Meg Greenfield captured this aspect of the Reagan approach:

> Someone told me the other day that the actor's way of doing things is only part of it with Reagan, that it is the onetime labor negotiator who is the real key. This has a certain plausibility: the long waiting-out of the adversary, the immobility meanwhile, the refusal to give anything until the last moment, the willingness—nonetheless—finally to yield to superior pressure or force or particular circumstance on almost everything, but only with something to show in return and only if the final deal can be interpreted as furthering the original Reagan objective.

All leaders would be well advised to carefully consider which parts of their responsibilities, including those for which they theoretically have direct authority or responsibility, could usefully be understood as negotiations. Strong negotiating skills are not only a key tool of leadership; in some cases they are *the* critical leadership skill.

REAGAN ON LEADERSHIP: NEGOTIATE FROM STRENGTH

- Become the negotiator-in-chief of your organization.

- Look over your organization's activities to determine which could be best viewed and handled as negotiations.

- Before entering a negotiation, lay the groundwork to define the terms of the discussion.

- Be patient. Wait for the other side to make offers, and do not be tempted to bid against yourself.

- Treat your opposite numbers with courtesy. Do not underestimate the importance of the personal contact between the leaders of both sides in reaching a mutually beneficial outcome.

- Do not attach your ego to a particular position or outcome.

- Listen carefully to what your adversary offers. Do not assume that you know in advance what he is offering. He may present ideas that you have not foreseen and that meet your goals as well or better than your own offer.

- While in negotiation, use your public statements to educate outsiders on the connection between your stance and your vision. Never discuss your negotiation tactics.

- After setting the strategy, have subordinates negotiate as far as they can, but be prepared to step in directly if necessary to conclude the agreement.

- Remember that negotiating techniques, as important as they are, are only as useful as the substantive result and its connection to your vision.

CHAPTER 4

KNOW WHEN TO APPLY AN INDIRECT APPROACH

A clever military leader will succeed in many cases in choosing defensive positions of such an offensive nature from the strategic point of view that the enemy is compelled to attack us in them.
—GRAF HELMUTH VON MOLTKE, CHIEF OF THE PRUSSIAN GENERAL STAFF

Gallant fellows, these soldiers; they always go for the thickest place in the fence.
—ADMIRAL JOHN DE ROBECK, WITNESSING THE SLAUGHTER OF BRITISH COMMONWEALTH TROOPS LANDING AT GALLIPOLI, APRIL 25, 1915

I T H A S L O N G been recognized—at least since the writings of the Chinese military theorist Sun-tzu more than 2,000 years ago—that goals are sometimes more readily accomplished by an indirect approach than by a direct approach.

The celebrated British military theorist Basil Liddell Hart updated and applied this theory to battles from ancient times through the 20th century in his classic work, *Strategy*. Though Liddell Hart had initially focused on its applicability to military strategy, he writes:

I began to realize that the indirect approach had a much wider application—that it was a law of life in all spheres: a truth of philosophy. Its fulfillment was seen to be the key to practical achievement in dealing with any problem where the human factor predominates, and a conflict of wills tends to spring from an underlying concern for interests. In all such cases, the direct assault of new ideas provokes a stubborn resistance, thus intensifying the difficulty of producing a change in outlook. Conversion is achieved more easily and rapidly by unsuspected infiltration of a different idea or argument that turns the flank of the instinctive opposition. The indirect approach is as fundamental to the realm of politics as to the realm of sex. In commerce, the suggestion that there is a bargain to be secured is far more potent than any direct appeal to buy. . . . As in war, the aim is to weaken resistance before attempting to overcome it; and the effect is best attained by drawing the other party out of his defences.

Reagan seemed to grasp this phenomenon instinctively. For example, as a young man he set his sights on becoming an actor. Though by his own account he had "fantasized" about acting in movies since he was a small child, he was careful not to share this goal with others:

> By my senior year at Eureka, my secret dream to be an actor was firmly planted, but I knew that in the middle of Illinois in 1932, I couldn't go around saying, "I want to be an actor."
>
> To say I wanted to be a movie star would have been as eccentric as saying I wanted to go to the moon. Hollywood and Broadway were at least as remote from Dixon as the moon was in 1932. If I *had* told anyone I was setting out to be a movie star, they'd have carted me off to an institution.

Reagan did not try to move to Hollywood at the first opportunity. He thought the best way to break through there might be through radio. With that in mind he first looked toward Chicago, "the hub of radio broadcasting." Facing tough prospects as the Great Depression gripped the nation, Reagan sought advice wherever he could get it. He approached a businessman who seemed to have contacts in various fields:

> I couldn't bring myself to tell him I wanted to go into the world of entertainment. I knew it would have sounded ridiculous. . . . Although I couldn't bring myself to mention acting, I . . . said: "I have to tell you, way down deep inside, what I'd really like to be is a radio sports announcer." (I'd seen several movies in which sports announcers played themselves and thought there was a remote possibility the job might lead me into the movies.)

The businessman advised Reagan to take an additional step back from directly seeking his goal. He suggested that Reagan not even mention sports announcing, but simply seek whatever job might be available in the new radio industry.

Ultimately, of course, Reagan found his way to Hollywood. But his route was far more circuitous and indirect than direct. After being turned down in his initial bid for a radio job in Chicago, he found a position in Davenport, Iowa—which he soon lost but later recovered—and then spent four years at a radio station in Des Moines. He began vacationing in Southern California in 1935, and in 1937, while covering the Chicago Cubs training camp at Pasadena, Reagan obtained the screen test that launched his film career.

Reagan's view of the indirect approach was also implicit in his negotiating style, as seen in the previous chapter. His actual goals, his bottom lines or "hole cards," were generally different from his initial bargaining position—and more limited.

His entire approach to nuclear arms control negotiation with the Soviet Union—build up in order to bargain away— could be viewed as an indirect approach. Even though he was open about his strategy, many did not take it at face value until very late in the process.

Reagan also tended to take an indirect approach in other situations. As a young Hollywood actor, he became dissatisfied with the decisions being made by executives guiding his career. At first, he did not confront his superiors directly. He decided that he would write a screenplay and then suggest himself for the lead role. Though this plan was not carried out, he did talk with other actors, as well as screenwriters, about his intentions.

Reagan even applied what might be considered an indirect approach in several of his bids for elective office. He would generally delay announcements of candidacy until he could point to an apparent public demand for his entry. Without question, however, the most significant issue on which he took an indirect approach was his use of the federal budget deficit, which ballooned during his presidency, as a lever against continued growth in government.

REAGAN'S APPROACH TO THE DEFICIT

*We must all realize that the deficit problem is
also an opportunity, an opportunity to construct a
new, leaner, better focused Federal structure.*
—RONALD REAGAN, PRESIDENT'S
BUDGET MESSAGE, 1986

*It is impossible to persuade Congress that expenditures must
be reduced, unless one creates deficits so large that absolutely
everyone becomes convinced that no more money can be spent.*
—FRIEDRICH HAYEK

When he took office in January 1981, Reagan had committed to several major policies with implications for national government spending. He had campaigned on a promise to dramatically increase defense spending, well above already significant increases belatedly sought by Carter as his term came to a close. He also committed to cut income taxes, which many in both political parties believed had risen too high as a result of inflation (the tax rates were not at that time indexed to inflation). He would protect the "entitlement" programs, particularly Social Security and Medicare, which consumed a huge and rapidly growing share of domestic federal spending. And he would do all this while rapidly reducing the federal budget deficit to zero, relying on spending cuts focused on "waste, fraud and abuse," and assuming revenue increases from an economy strengthened by tax cuts.

This combination of policies was famously termed "voodoo economics" by candidate George Bush, who later became Reagan's vice president. Others termed it "supply side economics," referring to its reliance on enhanced economic vitality through tax cuts. During the continuing recession of 1981–82, political opponents took to calling it "Reaganomics." As Reagan himself never tired of pointing out, once economic prosperity returned, continuing for a record amount of time—virtually unabated through the next decade—they stopped calling it Reaganomics.

For purposes of understanding his leadership and management techniques, our focus is not on the wisdom of the program, but on how Reagan approached goals that were, at least in the short term, competing. This is a problem, of course, that is in no way limited to political leaders; it is endemic to leadership in all realms. And it should be remembered that even if leaders do not begin an undertaking with competing priorities, circumstances may impose them.

Reagan, like other leading Republicans of his time, had a long commitment to balancing the federal budget. Indeed it was one of his key points of criticism of the administrations that preceded his own. As he sought the presidency in 1980, he nonetheless made clear that it was not the sole priority, much less the top priority. As he recalled:

> During the campaign, the people of America had told me nothing mattered more to them than national security. Time and again, when I went around the country calling for a balanced budget, I'd get this question: "But what if it comes down to a choice between national security and the deficit?"
>
> Every time, I answered: "I'd have to come down on the side of national defense." And every time I did, the audience roared. Nobody wanted a second-class army, navy, or air force defending our country.

He added, "My faith was in those tax reforms, and I believed we could have a balanced budget within two or three years—by 1984 at the latest."

While it was necessary for Reagan to convince the public that the nation's defenses were in disrepair, he did not have to persuade them that the economy also required urgent attention: "In 1981, no problem the country faced was more serious than the economic crisis—not even the need to modernize our armed forces—because without a recovery, we couldn't afford to do the things necessary to make the country strong again or make a serious effort to lessen the dangers of nuclear war. Nor could America regain confidence."

Against these two top priorities, the deficit took a distant back seat. As a result, the budget hemorrhaged red ink. Even when the economy turned around, beginning in 1983, Reagan did not act to change the budgetary priorities that were causing the deficits. The most significant areas of government spending that might theoretically be reduced—the entitlements—were off the table. The public had demonstrated, through their congressional representatives and in handfuls of polls, that this area was nonnegotiable. Reagan heeded this message, particularly after being scalded following his budget director's exploration of Social Security adjustments in 1981. The only other option to slash the short-term budget deficit was to abandon, or certainly imperil, one or both of his twin priorities of tax cuts and defense spending increases. Nonetheless, after he had compromised the tax cut principle, agreeing to significant hikes in 1982 in exchange for subsequent budget reductions, he found that Congress was not, as a practical matter, able to meet its commitments. Adding to the complexity, Reagan understood that the instability that would result from any abrupt policy change might have additional unforeseen negative consequences. As he found in the 1982 recession, in which strict monetary policies "wrung out" inflationary expectations from the economy, recessions increased the deficit because of the increased costs of assistance to those thrown into need.

Under these circumstances, working from his assumptions, a direct approach to effective deficit reduction was not a realistic option. Instead, Reagan took an indirect approach.

First, he maintained his rhetorical commitment to budget deficit reduction. Given the power of the presidential bully pulpit and his unique ability to use it, this allowed him to set the terms of the public debate. Reagan formulated the issue so as to bolster his own priorities: "Deficits, as I've often said, aren't caused by too little taxing, they are caused by too much spending." Actually, deficits are simply the gap between spending and taxing; they could presumably be erased by either increased taxation or decreased spending, or some combination. Reagan's approach, stated as a principle, was consistent with general public support for deciding how to spend their own money, rather than having government institutions decide. He was working to ensure that the public linked deficit reduction with the policy of limiting government spending and cutting its growth.

Second, stymied by successive sessions of Congress in his attempts at major spending reductions, Reagan concluded that the problem was structural. He was persuaded that the only way to get the Congress to stop its habitual reliance on deficit spending, year in and year out, was to enact two constitutional amendments to alter the incentives it faced. The first would require Congress to pass balanced budgets. The second would provide the president with line-item veto authority, allowing him to veto specific pork barrel appropriations that wasted federal funds. Otherwise, presidents in recent years (particularly after Congress imposed limitations on executive power to redirect spending in the 1970s) were limited to the unenviable choice of either vetoing an entire appropriation bill to stop the objectionable bits or signing the larger bill despite unjustified burdens on the taxpayer.

Third, Reagan continued to work to cut government spending in those areas not encompassed in the rubrics of defense or domestic entitlements. One of his techniques, which he had applied successfully as governor of California, was to bring in experts from the world of business to examine and recommend changes to government bureaucracies. The federal effort, called the Grace Commission, identified numerous areas where savings could be obtained. Of about 2,500 recommendations, nearly 800 were fully implemented, resulting in significant savings.

The commission approach also provided Reagan with other advantages. It provided him, and the public, with information about outdated or inefficient bureaucratic practices that might otherwise have gone undetected. This reinforced the principle of deficit reduction through spending cuts rather than tax increases. After all, who would favor increases to fund such waste as the experts identified?

It also had useful aspects for public communications. By supplying a stream of specific recommendations for savings, it reinforced his public message, maintaining momentum for cutting the deficit. In part, this may have built on the insight Reagan had years before about what he called "the psychology of audiences." Referring to his experience as governor, he later explained:

> As we started to make some headway in trimming costs, I began telling the public about the savings we were making and I learned it can be difficult for many people to envision a hundred million dollars or even one million for that matter.
>
> I'd mention an example of something we'd done that saved several million dollars and would get a glassy stare and polite applause.
>
> But during one speech to a group of business and professional people in San Francisco, I happened to mention that we'd been able to save about $200,000 by sending motorists their annual automobile registration renewal notices several weeks earlier than in the past; postal rates were going up and so we rushed to do our mailing before the increase went into effect. Well, after I said that, the audience came to their feet with a roar of approval. Two hundred thousand dollars they could visualize. Two hundred million, they couldn't.

Of course, anecdotes like this one can only be effective when they are consistent with the larger story they are intended to illustrate.

Finally, the combination of high deficits created by policy decisions and the continued commitment to reduce deficit spending shifted power within the administration from its operating agencies to the White House itself. The tremendous pressure on spending in the programs outside defense and favored entitlements transformed virtually all their policy decisions into budgetary decisions. This greatly enhanced the power of the Office of Management and Budget, which works directly for the president. Combined with separate, ongoing efforts to cut regulations, the budget pressure provided a powerful presidential counterweight to the general tendency of executive agencies to gravitate toward the views of their own bureaucracies, outside lobbying interests, and relevant congressional committees. Reagan's emphasis on deficit reduction constituted a masterful indirect approach to adding pressure on Congress to reduce domestic spending while continuing Reagan's other top priorities.

Some of his opponents saw the trap coming, perhaps before Reagan himself grasped the opportunity. In 1983, Senator Daniel Patrick Moynihan, a Democrat from New York, foresaw the political consequences of the mounting deficits:

> This accumulation of a serious debt . . . is all happening without any great public protest, or apparent political cost. . . . Under these circumstances, the only thing a Republican Administration and a Republican Senate will be able to consider doing will be to revert to their original agenda: use the budget deficit to force massive reductions in social programs. This time they will be able to cite not mere illusions but necessity. Even if interest on the debt climbs to $200 billion a year, as now seems likely, presumably there will still be an Army, an FBI, and some kind of customs service and border control. What then will be left to cut?
>
> Entitlements, or more precisely, Social Security.

It is unlikely that Moynihan was correct in his assertion that "there was a hidden agenda. . . . [Reagan] was astute enough to know there are constituencies for such activities, and he thought it would be pointless to try to argue them out of existence one by one. He would instead create a fiscal crisis in which, willy-nilly, they would be driven out of existence." His heavy reliance on Reagan's 1981 statement—"Well, you know, we can lecture our children about extravagance until we run out of voice and breath. Or we can cut their extravagance by simply reducing their allowance"—is not persuasive in the face of strong evidence to the contrary from top Reagan economic advisers such as Martin Anderson.

On the other hand, there is no question that the increased deficit did become the core of a powerful indirect approach to cut domestic spending. Allan H. Ryskind, editor of one of Reagan's favorite publications, the conservative weekly *Human Events,* observed in 1988: "It has certainly put a lid on the welfare state. The Democrats have sort of trapped themselves because they've said this is all terrible and horrible and that closing the deficit should be the first priority. The fact that they've said the deficit is such a problem, prevents them from proposing new spending programs."

Reagan's combination of increasing deficits at the same time that he increased public support for cutting government spending had far-reaching consequences. Major candidates for the presidency, as well as lesser offices, increasingly voiced support for a constitutional amendment to balance the budget. Reagan's successors, Democrat Clinton as well as Republican Bush, continued to advocate Reagan's favored Line Item Veto Act. When it was finally enacted, it included a proviso that it was only to be exercised to reduce the budget deficit; it is not to be used when the budget is balanced or in surplus. Similarly, the landmark Budget Enforcement Act of 1990, requiring that legislated entitlement increases or revenue losses be offset elsewhere in the budget, only applies if the proposed legislation "increases the deficit."

The success of Reagan's indirect approach is striking. By the late 1990s, both liberals and conservatives habitually pay obeisance to the necessity of balanced federal budgets. They also tend to focus on cutting spending rather than increasing taxes. Indeed, some Republicans in Congress relied so heavily for so long on the existence of the deficit as their rationale for cutting government that they have been disoriented as the deficit has shrunk and begun to show signs of moving into surplus.

It remains unclear how Reagan came to this approach. One recalls Martin Anderson's observation about Reagan's tendency to seek much more in negotiation than he would expect or receive: "This was never acknowledged, perhaps even to himself." Whether he consciously chose the indirect approach or came to it by serendipitous circumstance, his use of the deficit to redirect the taxing and spending incentives facing the national government was an extraordinary example of the power of the indirect approach. Leaders facing obstacles to a direct approach to accomplishing their top priorities or coping with incompatibility among their priorities can find much worthy of consideration in Reagan's example.

REAGAN ON LEADERSHIP: KNOW WHEN TO APPLY AN INDIRECT APPROACH

- When a direct approach has small likelihood of success, consider whether an indirect approach can be more effective.

- An indirect approach can be most effective if the leader generally follows a direct approach; it then includes elements of surprise and unpredictability.

- Remember von Moltke's dictum: If you can lead your opponent into attacking you when you have assumed defensive positions with an offensive nature, you may succeed more rapidly than if you had sparked a direct confrontation.

- Do not be afraid for opponents to seize your arguments; welcome it.

- If committed to incompatible priorities, consider ancillary benefits that might accrue from an indirect approach to achieving one. For example, recall how the increasing deficit allowed Reagan's administration to exert additional controls on operating agencies through an invigorated budget review process.

- When using an indirect approach, take care to maintain it within your vision. Recall Reagan's rhetorical offensive for new tools to balance the budget at the very time the deficits swelled on his watch. Also recall that it was consistent with his campaign commitments as to priorities.

- In deciding whether to pursue a goal through an indirect strategy, consider what the appropriate time frame for accomplishment should be. A fundamental choice Reagan made was to deal with the deficit on a longer time horizon than his other priorities.

- Remember: The bottom line is results. There is no wisdom in going for the thickest place in the fence unless it is the best way to achieve your goal.

CHAPTER 5

LEARN FROM FAILURE AND MISTAKES— AND MOVE ON

Now, what should happen when you make a mistake is this:
You take your knocks, you learn your lessons, and then you
move on. That's the healthiest way to deal with a problem.
—RONALD REAGAN, ADDRESS TO THE NATION ON THE
TOWER COMMISSION REPORT, MARCH 4, 1987

E VERY ORGANIZATION, like every individual, will make mistakes. It is equally predictable that all will face failures, which in some cases will result from mistakes and in others from circumstances beyond anyone's reasonable control or foresight.

What is less predictable is how people recover from mistakes and failure. Some people overcome repeated disappointments and setbacks, while others break and disappear from the scene.

The key is not the objective circumstances, but how one views the circumstances. Reagan not only accepted the inevitability of mistakes and failures; he saw America's tolerance for second chances—and Americans' willingness to try again —as one of our nation's great strengths. Speaking to Russian students in 1988, he explained:

> The explorers of the modern era are the entrepreneurs, men with vision, with the courage to take risks and faith enough to brave the unknown. . . . Some people, even in my own country, look at the riot of experiment that is the free market and see only waste. What of all the entrepreneurs that fail? Well, many do, particularly the successful ones; often several times. And if you ask them the secret of their success, they'll tell you it's all they learned in their struggles along the way; yes, it's what they learned from failing. Like an athlete in competition or a scholar in pursuit of the truth, experience is the greatest teacher.

Experience may be the greatest teacher, but as in all educational transactions, the willingness to learn is equally important. Some companies, recognizing the potential benefits of learning from errors, encourage innovation among their employees by ensuring soft landings for strong performers who make mistakes.

Leaders confront especially acute challenges from mistakes and failure. The greater the enterprise for which they are accountable, the higher the stakes. In a business, the consequences of a strategic error could be lost jobs, both inside and outside the company, with disruption or damage to individuals and families. In a government, at the highest levels the results can be catastrophic, including loss of life.

In recent years there have been numerous opportunities to observe how leaders handle failure and mistakes. Some have been at the highest political levels, with consequences at home and through the world, at the time and well into the future. The Vietnam conflict and the Watergate scandal are the most pungent examples. Others have occurred in the corporate world. Examples include Ford Motor Company's introduction of the Edsel and Coca Cola's "New Coke" fiasco; the rise and demise of eight-track audiotapes and the Betamax video cassette; the poisonings linked to *E. coli* contamination of meat and adulterated Tylenol capsules.

Given the certainty that mistakes and failures will occur—but the unpredictability of just how, when, and where they will occur, and what form they will take—many enterprises now take the wise step of methodically planning their response in advance. One increasingly common step is to have "crisis communications" drills, to ensure that key groups (such as the general public, the news media, investors, regulators, competitors, customers, and suppliers) will be able to learn what is actually happening and so maintain confidence. Some also go through "crisis management" drills. These not only practice the management response under simulated crisis conditions; they can also highlight otherwise hidden dysfunctions that may be increasing the likelihood that mistakes will be made in the first place.

Leaders who successfully handle mistakes and failures tend to take six steps. First the failure or mistake must be acknowledged. This might appear self-evident in the abstract, but in practice it may not be an obvious call. The leader must then assume accountability for the mishap as well as its aftermath. At that point, the leader should disclose all relevant information to interested and affected parties. He should make certain that the cause of the mistake or failure is fully understood and implement changes to ensure that the organization has learned from the error. Finally, less visible to others but critically important for the leader and the organization, he must turn his back on the past and move ahead without having his confidence impaired.

ACKNOWLEDGE MISTAKES OR FAILURES

At one level this seems so apparent as to be trivial. In practice, it can be a very difficult decision—and one that draws heavily upon the leader's personal strengths. He will have to rely on his knowledge, experience, and perhaps most important, his instinct.

In some situations, failure is self-evident. In such cases the military maxim holds: "Never reinforce failure." Reagan faced this situation after the terrorist bombing in Lebanon in 1983. The loss of 241 marines was not only tragic, it appeared unnecessary. The absence of a clear mission for our armed forces there had been exposed in the most terrible way. Although Reagan initially authorized military retaliation, he soon acceded to the near consensus of his advisers that withdrawal—the administration preferred to call it "redeployment to the sea"—was the best option. As with any military failure, a key leadership challenge is to acknowledge that the enterprise was a mistake while not breaking morale and leaving people to conclude that the loss of lives was pointless.

A leadership issue of a different kind arose during the dark days of the 1981–82 recession. The question was whether the Reagan economic policy, begun the previous year, was a mistake that had caused or prolonged the recession. Many people, including supporters as well as opponents of his administration, pressed Reagan to alter or abandon his economic plan. Reagan rejected the advice, urging that insufficient time had passed to conclude that it had failed. Under his formulation, the recession was a lagging consequence of policies followed prior to his election. The best way forward would be to "stay the course" on which he was moving the nation. As events unfolded, prosperity soon emerged and his approach was vindicated in the public mind. Reagan's measure of whether a failure had occurred—in this case the relevant time frame—differed from that offered by those who sought to classify the policy as mistaken.

Reagan had a similar experience in foreign policy, when he focused on building arms as a means to negotiating arms reduction. As he later wrote:

> There were certain parallels in the situations regarding our economic recovery program and my attempts to get the Russians to the bargaining table. . . . The balance in the arms race had already changed and I was certain it was going to get the Russians' attention. But, as with the economy, there was a lag time before the full impact of the new policy was apparent. *And there were people who said it wasn't working;* there was pressure throughout that year to abandon the policy, forget the MX and peace through strength, and try something new with the Russians—which to many of my critics simply meant appeasement.
>
> As with my economic recovery program, I felt sure the new national security policies—if they were given time—would work. My instructions to our national security team were the same as I'd given to those working for an economic turnaround: Hang tough and stay the course.

As in economic policy, Reagan's stance was later vindicated through the achievement of tangible results.

The most notable policy mistake of the Reagan presidency was the so-called Iran-Contra affair. The crippling flaws in policy and judgment that underlay this scandal are obvious in even the briefest summary. The first branch of the scandal arose from efforts to obtain the freedom of American hostages in the Middle East, working in collusion with Iran, to whom the United States would sell arms. No matter what the context, the notion of arms for hostages went against national policy. Also important from a leadership perspective, it flew in the face of public expectations of Reagan. The second part of the scandal involved the diversion of money from the arms sales to the Nicaraguan Contras, who were fighting the Sandanista regime. Putting aside the source of the fund-ing, such aid was intended to circumvent public accountability in general, and in particular to artfully skirt statutory limitations on U.S. aid to the Contras.

Reagan's instincts—bolstered by several aides who would later be prosecuted for their attempts to cover up the scandal—led him initially to resist accountability. In the midst of cascading revelations, he spoke to the nation on November 13, 1986. He defended the secret contacts with Iran, arguing that they did not constitute an arms-for-hostages transaction. Negotiating with the Iranian intermediaries was not the same as dealing with the terrorists, Reagan believed. As he reiterated in his memoirs, "If your child was kidnapped and someone who wasn't the kidnapper came to you and offered to help you find your child, I think most parents would take that help even if it cost you some money."

Reagan, who took great pride in his ability to communicate with the American people, had been reluctant to give the speech. His reluctance was justified in the negative public reaction; people simply did not believe him. As Lou Cannon wrote, "Reagan was on this night a carping, angry, and defensive politician who blamed the media for his troubles much like any other cornered politician."

Finally, in a televised address on March 4, 1987, Reagan directly acknowledged the mistake at the heart of the controversy:

A few months ago I told the American people I did not trade arms for hostages. My heart and my best intentions still tell me that's true, but the facts and evidence tell me it is not. As the Tower Board reported, what began as a strategic opening to Iran deteriorated, in its implementation, into trading arms

for hostages. This runs counter to my own beliefs, to administration policy, and to the original strategy we had in mind. It was
a mistake.

ASSUME ACCOUNTABILITY

For the leader to acknowledge the mistake is the critical first
step, but it is only the first step. This is illustrated by what
might be called the Khrushchev approach.

During an exchange between the then–Soviet premier and
President John F. Kennedy, the American asked, "Do you ever
admit a mistake?"

The cagey Russian responded, "Certainly I do. In a speech
before the Twentieth Party Congress, I admitted all of Stalin's
mistakes."

While all can see the humor in Khrushchev's answer, some
leaders may also see themselves. We have already noted how
subordinates, doubtless in large part out of selfish motivations, sought to mislead Reagan on the nature of the Iran arms
negotiation; they did not want him to publicly acknowledge
the policy as a failure. At the next decision point, whether the
leader should assume accountability, subordinates whose positions are closely linked to the person in charge might urge an
attempt to shift accountability in an effort to protect themselves. Yet again, the casualty could be trust, both inside and
outside the enterprise.

President Kennedy did not follow the Khrushchev approach in the aftermath of the Bay of Pigs imbroglio, which
occurred at the beginning of his administration in 1961. American military power, in an eerie harbinger of the Vietnam
struggle to come, was defeated in an attempt to incite the over-
throw of Fidel Castro. Mistakes were made at every level:
Strategic and tactical military decisions were flawed, intelli-

gence data were incomplete, the political leadership was irresolute. That the result was failure was unmistakable—the entire world witnessed it. Kennedy might have rationalized the failure and his responsibility for it, seeking refuge in the complexities and ambiguities he had faced in authorizing the mission. Instead, he decisively cut to the chase and publicly assumed accountability. Surprising many, his support among the American people rose as a result.

Reagan took this approach in his address on March 4, 1987:

> I take full responsibility for my own actions and for those of my administration. As angry as I may be about activities taken without my knowledge, I am still accountable for those activities. As disappointed as I may be in some who served me, I'm still the one who must answer to the American people for this behavior. And as personally distasteful as I find secret bank accounts and diverted funds—well, as the Navy would say, this happened on my watch.

The complexity, secrecy, and convoluted nature of the misbegotten policy at the heart of the scandal were beyond the ken of most viewers; they had enough to do in their own lives. But everyone can understand what is involved in the leader's personal assumption of accountability for a situation that includes mistakes and failures and is at variance with his vision, record, and commitments. This was the critical first step in restoring public trust after a public failure.

OPEN YOUR BOOKS

In the aftermath of a failure or mistake, the leader must not only work to contain the direct damage to the organization or to others that may have occurred but also—and it may be at least as important—work to reestablish the credibility of the leader and the enterprise. The best way to restore trust is to prove oneself trustworthy, and the best way to prove oneself trustworthy is to share all relevant information.

This approach may hold significant practical risk. A company may be concerned about disclosing proprietary information. A government may have reasonable concerns about the immediate or long-term consequences arising from pulling back veils of secrecy. Additional concerns may be raised in government about misuse of information by political opponents or a hostile press. In the private sector competitors and the press may occasion analogous fears. In all settings, lawyers representing organizations or individuals facing potential civil or criminal liability will predictably advise against broad disclosures.

Such concerns may be most forcefully pressed when the need to overrule them is greatest, because the magnitude of the mistake or failure requires decisive action to restore trust. Under such circumstances, the leader should lean heavily toward opening the books.

Early in the public exposure of the Iran-Contra scandal, during the period before Reagan publicly acknowledged error, he nonetheless initiated fact-finding efforts. On December 1, 1986, he appointed a special review panel, known as the Tower Commission, which comprised two respected former senators and a former White House national security adviser. In December, following an internal inquiry led by the attorney general with Reagan's approval, the attorney general took steps that culminated in the appointment of an independent counsel on December 19, 1986. The latter step was taken despite the administration's long-standing, publicly stated legal objections to the statute under which the independent counsel was appointed. In this period Reagan also appointed a respected former ambassador to assist in the laborious but critical task of gathering and organizing the voluminous documents at issue in executive, congressional, and independent counsel inquiries.

On March 4, 1987, when Reagan did acknowledge error and assume accountability, his credibility was bolstered by the existence of these efforts. The fact that the Tower Commission report had been highly critical of White House management practices added credibility to its finding, which Reagan quoted in his speech: "The Board is convinced that the President does indeed want the full story to be told."

TAKE REMEDIAL ACTION

For the leader's assumption of accountability to have meaning to its audience, it must be linked to measurable steps to correct the situation that led to the mistake in the first instance. Reagan's speech of March 4, 1987, was also strong on this score.

Reagan committed to taking action in three areas, which he broke down along lines of personnel, national security policy, and the national security policy decision process. With respect to personnel, he announced major changes. He had recently recruited the highly respected former senator Howard Baker as chief of staff. Baker probably brought more independent stature to the position than anyone else in history; he also had a reputation for probity that transcended partisan divisions. His credibility—and the president's—was enhanced by his renunciation of aspirations for 1988, when he could surely have been a strong potential presidential candidate in his own right. Reagan also brought new blood to other positions implicated in the Iran-Contra debacle: the national security adviser post and the directorship of the Central Intelligence Agency.

To correct the national security policy breakdown, he ordered a "comprehensive review of all covert operations," to ensure that they would be "in support of clear policy objectives and in compliance with American values." Most relevant, he also "issued a directive prohibiting the NSC staff itself from undertaking covert operations—no ifs, ands, or buts."

Finally, Reagan agreed to accept the recommendations of the Tower Commission for reforming the National Security Council's decision process. He tasked the new national security adviser with "reporting back to me on further reforms that might be needed."

REGAIN CONFIDENCE AND MOVE ON

In the aftermath of Reagan's March 4 address, his public support rapidly increased and he recovered much of the ground lost the previous winter. Also important, major opinion leaders such as the *Washington Post* editorial page were satisfied that the president was putting the crisis behind him. They were prepared to let him move on. Richard Neustadt, looking back in 1990, added perspective to his examination of the Iran-Contra story: "It dominates this chapter in a way it will not dominate his history. For Reagan recovered from it. Indeed, the recovery is a success story."

Reagan did indeed recover, making history in his final two years of office, especially in nuclear arms control. And he left office with record levels of popularity. But the recovery was not entirely the result of the actions he took that culminated in the address of March 4, 1987.

Another key was his ability to put the matter behind him. Why some individuals crumple after a serious mistake while others bounce back is of course mysterious and complex. Winston Churchill, who had numerous mistakes and failures during his long public career, famously came back again and again. He was able to do this even though several of his decisions undoubtedly occasioned horrific damage. In the First World War, the invasion of Gallipoli was a strategically bold attempt to end the gruesome and apparently interminable slaughter on the western front by opening a second front through Turkey. Although Churchill would always defend the conception of this operation, it was undoubtedly a failure in execution that occurred on his watch. The Allied powers suffered more than a quarter of a million casualties as a result.

Churchill later moved from matters of life and death to those of bread and butter. His pivotal role in returning Britain to the gold standard in the 1920s is almost universally viewed as a calamitous error, leading to unnecessary privation among millions of his countrymen.

What is more, both of these decisions were well known everywhere. Churchill lost office over the Gallipoli catastrophe, retreated to the front in France, dedicated much of his subsequent World War I memoir to defending his actions, and in future years continued to face hecklers who raised it in public meetings. His action with respect to the gold standard was immortalized by John Maynard Keynes' eloquent and lethal pamphlet, "The Economic Consequences of Mr. Churchill."

As we all know, Churchill overcame these and other mistakes and failures to lead his nation and the world with unmatched heroism and effectiveness in the Second World War. His famous "shock absorber" somehow got him through.

Thankfully, Reagan faced nothing as catastrophic as Gallipoli. Nonetheless, the Beirut bombing preyed heavily on him. He later wrote, "The sending of the marines to Beirut was the source of my greatest regret and my greatest sorrow as president. . . . Every day since the death of those boys, I have prayed for them and their loved ones." He did try to take the lessons learned from reflection on the tragic loss in Lebanon and apply them to policy to prevent a recurrence. This apparently allowed him to move on.

The steady stream of public revelations arising from the Iran-Contra affair presented a different sort of challenge; for Reagan personally, his own loss of credibility with the American people may have been the hardest blow. Reagan denied that his office was "paralyzed" as public concern mounted to the unraveling of the Iran-Contra affair. He later explained:

> Those first months after the Iran-Contra affair hit the front pages were frustrating for me. For the first time in my life, people didn't believe me. I had told the truth, but they still didn't believe me. While I was unhappy, I never felt depressed about the situation: There wasn't a gloom or "malaise" hanging over the Oval Office, as some writers have suggested. I just went on with my job. . . . But if I wasn't depressed about what was going on, I sure felt frustrated that I couldn't get my message across.

For our purposes what is interesting is not so much the reality of the mood in the White House, but Reagan's description of his approach. Though he understood and regretted that accomplishments in his final two years were made more difficult as a result of the scandal, he followed his own advice and "moved on." He believed that the Tower Commission report had cleared reasonable doubts about his credibility. Doubtless satisfied that the March 4 speech had in large part restored his rapport with the American people, he gave no appearance of fixating or obsessing on the mistakes that had been made.

While no one can get inside someone else's mind, one can observe patterns of behavior that reflect habits of thought.

Reagan's approach to the Iran-Contra setback mirrored his description, in another context, of his mother's advice to him growing up: "If something went wrong, she said, you didn't let it get you down: You stepped away from it, stepped over it, and moved on. Later on, she added, something good will happen and you'll find yourself thinking—'If I hadn't had that problem back then, then this better thing that *did* happen wouldn't have happened to me.'"

Throughout his life, Reagan would "move on." By his own account he seemed to recover rapidly from his failure to obtain an early career toehold in Chicago, from not being selected for a coveted job with Montgomery Ward, from being fired from his first job as a radio announcer. In the early 1950s, following years of success as a film actor, he had a dry streak. He had a period of more than a year where he appeared in no movies. He did some television appearances, which were then viewed as risky for actors. Memorably, he even emceed a Las Vegas show featuring a group called the Continentals but decided after two weeks that he did not feel comfortable in "smoke-filled nightclubs." Soon, however, Reagan's career took a positive if unanticipated turn when he was approached to host *General Electric Theater,* an extremely successful television program.

In his political career as well, he appeared to bounce back quickly and move on. Following his excruciatingly narrow defeat for the Republican nomination for president in 1976, as well as defeats in primaries and caucuses in the 1976 and 1980 campaigns, there is no evidence that Reagan became obsessed with failures or mistakes.

The same appears to have been the case in his personal life, though his lack of public introspection makes for less certainty. In his memoirs he wrote of being "shattered" by the breakup of his engagement to his long-time girlfriend Margaret Cleaver. Nonetheless, "something inside me suggested

that things would work out all right." By all accounts he was
initially devastated after the breakup of his first marriage,
years later, to actress Jane Wyman (their separation was pre-
saged, after one day, by the death of a baby girl born four
months prematurely). Perhaps as a sign he had fully "moved
on," Reagan did not even mention Wyman or the marriage in
an early draft of his memoirs. At the request of an editor he
later added four sentences, containing the barest facts. The
editor, Michael Korda, later recounted this incident, speculating that the omission might have reflected the views of
Reagan's second wife, Nancy. Nonetheless the omission would
be consistent with his approach of "moving on."

In their book *When Smart People Fail,* Carole Hyatt and
Linda Gottlieb recommend that people carefully, consciously,
deliberately reinterpret failures and mistakes to make positive
use of them. Then, as they move forward, they should make an
effort to label themselves and their experiences in a positive
way that bolsters rather than undercuts their self-confidence.
Whether from his mother's advice or other sources—such as
his means of coping with his father's alcoholism—Reagan
appears to have taken this approach.

What emerged was a pattern of relentless focusing on the
positive, even in the face of major failures and mistakes. Lou
Cannon concluded that Reagan's attitude of optimism could
lead him in some cases to rationalize misjudgments. Cannon
includes Reagan's continuing belief in his own innocence in
the Iran-Contra affair as an example. What is clear is that once
he did admit error, acknowledge accountability, disclose the
facts, and take action, he was then able to move ahead. As in
other examples of failures or mistakes in his life, he did not
allow them to redefine his view of himself, impairing his
self-confidence.

One reason that people react with a lack of trust when a
leader fails to acknowledge an error may be an almost instinc-

tive sense that the leader is protecting his own self-image rather than looking out for the good of the enterprise. That is a sound instinct, since anyone whose self-image requires perfection may have numerous unresolved personal issues that could have serious consequences if magnified in a leadership position. Once acknowledgment occurs and remedial actions are taken, the confidence of others inside and outside the organization can hopefully be regained. It is equally important for a leader to restore his own self-confidence; he must move on if the enterprise is to move ahead. The relentless self-confidence and optimism that Reagan exhibited in such circumstances is an example worthy of emulation.

———◆———

REAGAN ON LEADERSHIP: LEARN FROM FAILURE AND MISTAKES—AND MOVE ON

- Every organization—and every individual—will make mistakes and face failure. To the maximum possible extent such events should be viewed as important opportunities to learn.

- Plan in advance for mistakes and failures; the only thing one can know for sure is that they will occur.

- Use care in determining if a failure or mistake has occurred; sometimes a situation may be susceptible to multiple interpretations based on the time frame considered or other variables.

- Never reinforce failure. Where a failure or a mistake has occurred, acknowledge it as soon as practicable.

- Assume accountability for the failure or mistake in order to begin to rebuild trust. While many may not understand the nature of the error, virtually everyone understands what is involved in personally assuming accountability for something that takes place "on your watch."

- Err on the side of providing too much rather than too little information in the aftermath of a mistake or failure.

- Take decisive remedial action in your organization that makes plain that lessons have been learned and changes are being made. The actions should be consistent with your overall vision and should bolster rather than contradict your personal assumption of accountability.

- Once you have taken these steps for your organization, be sure that you personally "move on" as well. Do not allow naysayers or negative habits of thought to cause your self-confidence to reflect misfortunes, mistakes, or failures rather than your abilities and achievements.

CHAPTER 6

COMING, GOING, AND TIMING

How about that timing?
—RONALD REAGAN, SPEAKING TO
STAFF AFTER DELIVERING
FIRESIDE CHAT ABOUT
TAX CUTS, 1981

Observe due measure, for right timing is in
all things the most important factor.
—HESIOD, "WORKS AND DAYS"

W<small>E ALL FACE</small> questions of timing in our lives. A momentary hesitation in an intimate discussion can have profound results in a personal relationship. A business decision, apparently wise on the merits, may be entirely overtaken by events. An action taken too soon or too late is a very different action from one taken on time.

As one might expect, given his success as a professional actor and public speaker, Ronald Reagan focused on timing as a key presentation skill. His gifted speechwriter, Kenneth Khachigian, recalls, "He had a great sense of timing. In a thirty-second spot he liked to come in at twenty-eight seconds, leaving time enough for a 'trailer' to be added. *It was almost like he had a clock in his head.*"

He also applied a keen, almost innate, sense of timing in other ways. As we saw in considering his decisiveness, Reagan would sometimes apply a longer time frame for judging the success or failure of a decision than was conventional. He did not assume that the deadline for judgment was a particular year, or an election, or some other date that someone else set; if he believed his policy on economic reform or negotiating with the Soviets required more time, he would stick with the clock in his head.

Reagan also recognized that how a leader initially assumes authority and how he ultimately departs are critical to the on-going effectiveness and future perceptions of his leadership. He understood that the stagecraft of timing, of coming and going, can have practical and significant effects on statecraft.

COMING

Reagan took great care in approaching the situations in which he was going to be introduced to the public in a new leader-ship role. He understood the importance of first impressions. Initial perceptions of a leader can set a tone that lasts far into the future, almost irrespective of intervening, contradictory events.

In the aftermath of his October 1964 nationally televised speech supporting Barry Goldwater's doomed presidential bid, Reagan became a hot political property. In California, where Republicans were divided between moderates and con-servatives, many people viewed him as having a unique poten-tial to bring people together. Then, with a united Republican party behind him, his boosters thought he might have a real-istic chance to defeat incumbent governor Pat Brown in the upcoming 1966 election. By all accounts, Reagan was initially resistant, citing his family life and concerns for privacy, his age, and satisfaction with his career in show business.

Reagan did not say yes or no immediately; instead he made an offer to his supporters:

> Even though I think you're wrong about my being the only Republican who might be able to beat Brown, if you fellows arrange it for me to go on the road and accept some of the speaking invitations I'm getting from groups around the state, then I'll go out and speak to them and come back in six months, on the last day of 1965, and tell whether you're right or whether you should be looking for somebody else to run for governor.
>
> I believed that if I continued speaking for six months I'd be able to identify someone whom the people thought would make a good governor, then I'd campaign for him. . . .
>
> After about three months of this, I returned home one night and said to Nancy, "This isn't working out the way I thought it would. You know, these guys may be right. All these people are telling me after my speeches that I ought to run for governor; this may end up putting us in an awful spot."

Many observers at the time thought that Reagan had in fact decided rather early during his fact-finding tour. Recalling a meeting during that period, Lyn Nofziger, then a newspaperman but later to become one of Reagan's top aides, wrote:

> It was a pleasant lunch, with Reagan denying that he had decided to run for anything. He said he was still exploring the possibility. I didn't believe him, however, and of course I was right, even though it was four months before he announced. Over the years, despite the urgings of staff and friends, Reagan always waited until the last possible moment to announce his candidacies, even when there was little doubt in anyone's mind, including his own, about his ultimate decision. He had an instinctive

feeling about what was right politically for him and it was almost impossible to budge him once he had made up his mind. So he announced pretty much on his own timetable, not the campaign management's, not even an astrologer's.

In the end, there is no question that his unusual approach was effective. It set him apart from many other politicians—also from many others seeking leadership positions in private life. It was clear that he regarded the issues at stake as more important than whether he held a particular office. It also reminded people generally of what he had already made clear to his early backers: He had some degree of ambivalence, and he certainly did not need the position in any sense. Obviously it would not be of financial benefit compared to what else he might do. He was not seeking office to gratify the ego needs that drive so many individuals. His recognized accomplishments in another field of endeavor, as well as his relatively advanced age for his first attempt at elective office, made that plain.

He relied on others approaching him for his assistance, rather than the other way around. With that premise, he was able to listen to interested people across California, without having his first exposure be as a candidate for governor who, it would be assumed, had a comprehensive plan at the tip of his tongue. Instead, he asked the people what they thought was important, reminding them that they were in charge—and that he understood they were in charge. This approach also allowed him to pursue many of the activities any politician would have to endure but without the taint of having it credibly dismissed as "political." If and when he did choose to run, it would be at least as much because of the desires of other people as of his own.

Throughout the remainder of his political career, Reagan would carefully orchestrate the timing of his entry into a campaign. In late 1983, as president, he openly discussed the point in response to the question of when he would announce whether he would seek reelection in 1984: "At the last possible moment that I can announce a decision, and for a very obvious reason. Number one, if the answer is no, I'm a lame duck and can't get anything done. If the answer is yes, they'll charge that everything I'm doing is political—and I can't get anything done. So, I'm going to wait as long as I can."

A political writer at the time noted that Reagan had even declined to reveal his intention to run to his closest advisers in the fall of 1983, sitting "as silent as a Trappist monk." In the end, he wrote, "Reagan's flair for the dramatic may have been a political masterstroke."

When he judged that a campaign announcement would be better served by different timing, he did not hesitate to take another approach. Looking ahead to the 1980 campaign for the presidency, he "dropped his characteristic coyness about his own intentions" and very early on began to send "distinct signals" that he would run. The difference was that many people apparently were presuming that his advancing age would keep him out of the race, and he did not want that perception to put him at a disadvantage.

Reagan also worked to make a strong impression on the public as he took office. He was sensitive to the dramatic possibilities of the rituals surrounding his taking the oath of office, followed by his inaugural address. For reasons that are not entirely clear, for example, when he first became governor in 1967, he was sworn in just after midnight. Later in the day he also presented a well-received address. However, after an intriguing start, his early days as governor were characterized more by drift than decisiveness. Having come to office in a nontraditional manner, he was bereft of some of the institutional pieces that would have allowed him to move the complex mass of government in the new direction he sought.

Without question, he missed a significant leadership opportunity at that time.

With the experience he had garnered in Sacramento, and having ultimately become a very effective governor, Reagan entered the presidency with a clear plan to strike hard and fast from day one. In the midst of the preceding campaign—in a situation where most candidates tend to avoid advance planning for fear of appearing overconfident—he authorized key planning actions that would allow the prospective administration to come off the blocks fast. A headhunting operation was established, identifying key personnel decisions as well as potential candidates. He also authorized drafting of a strategy for the first hundred days of the prospective administration, led by individuals who had worked with him in Sacramento and in private business. Following the November election, during the transition period before Reagan was to assume office on January 20, 1981, detailed briefings of his policy commitments and plans were provided to new and prospective members of the administration. These exercises translated the often broad promises made by a presidential candidate into the workaday world of the federal bureaucracy.

With these steps behind him, Reagan was in a strong position to take immediate action as soon as he assumed office. With the general public, key Washington insiders (ranging from the press to the Congress to lobbying groups representing various interests to foreign embassies), and other nations focused on the new administration, he would be able to signal change and decisiveness by his initial actions.

On his first day in office, in addition to delivering a powerful inaugural address, Reagan signed an executive order abolishing federal price controls on oil and gasoline. This was an unmistakable early signal that he would meet his campaign pledges, that his administration was taking a very different approach to the energy crisis from his predecessor's, and that he was willing to assume accountability for a decision that many publicly predicted would cause oil and gas prices for consumers to soar. On the following day, he abolished the Council on Wage and Price Stability, another relic of economic policies he was abandoning. He also took other steps to limit government hiring and otherwise lay the groundwork for his economic reform legislative package.

In foreign affairs he also sent signals that change was in the air. In his second week in office, the new president "deliberately set out to say some frank things about the Russians, to let them know there were some new fellows in Washington who had a realistic view of what they were up to and weren't going to let them keep it up." At his very first press conference—on January 29, 1981—he sent shock waves across the world:

> Well, so far détente's been a one-way street that the Soviet Union has used to pursue its own aims. I don't have to think of an answer as to what I think their intentions are; they have repeated it. I know of no leader of the Soviet Union since the revolution, and including the present leadership, that has not more than once repeated in the various Communist congresses they hold their determination that their goal must be the promotion of world revolution and a one-world Socialist or Communist state, whichever word you want to use.
>
> Now, as long as they do that and as long as they, at the same time, have openly and publicly declared that the only morality they recognize is what will further their cause, meaning they reserve unto themselves the right to commit any crime, to lie, to cheat, in order to attain that, and that is moral, not immoral, and we operate on a different set of standards. I think when you do business with them, even at a détente, you keep that in mind.

In his first year, Reagan also earned a reputation for effectiveness by achieving enactment of his economic recovery legislative package, focused largely on major tax cuts. Doubtless his administration was determined to achieve early victories in part by the chastening lesson of President Carter, whose legislative reputation had sunk very low by the end of his first year in office, never to recover. Reagan also recognized that even with a strong beginning, his ability to accomplish major changes on the legislative front would inevitably wane with the passage of time. His simultaneous rhetorical offensive against the Soviet Union marked the beginning of what he envisioned as long-running negotiations that would occupy most of his time in office. When added to the effect of unforeseen events, such as the public outpouring after the attempt on Reagan's life in March 1981 and the decisive response to the PATCO strike in August of that year, it is clear that his leadership was greatly strengthened by his team's early and methodical start.

GOING

Knowing how and when to leave the stage is every bit as important as knowing how and when to enter it. For leaders, as for others who perform before an audience such as professional athletes and actors, the end point is a critical point. Jerry Seinfeld, one of the most popular comedians of the 1990s, stunned the nation by his decision to end his hit television series in 1998:

> I felt . . . the Moment. That's the only way I can describe it. I just know from being onstage for years and years and years, there's one moment where you have to feel the audience is still having a great time, and if you get off right there, they walk out of the theater excited. And yet, if you wait a bit longer and try to give them more for their money, they walk out feeling not as good. If I get off now I have a chance at a standing ovation. That's what you go for.

Reagan, reflecting his experience as a professional actor and public speaker, thought in similar terms of giving his audiences good value. An example of his sense of the moment was his speech to the Republican National Convention at Kansas City, Missouri, on August 19, 1976. Having narrowly failed in his primary challenge against an incumbent president—and all of the machinery of government and party at the incumbent's direction—Reagan appeared calm, sitting high in the convention center with his wife, taking interviews from television reporters. As a demonstration by his supporters continued at length, he told reporters that he had no expectation of speaking to the convention. He waited until President Ford, having asked Reagan to address the convention in a show of unity, waved to him from the podium. Following a dramatic entrance, Reagan spoke eloquently of his vision and of the party's victory in hoisting a platform "banner of bold unmistakable colors with no pale pastel shades."

While this was in one sense a farewell address, at least to the 1976 race, Reagan's skillful presentation, moving beyond any public expression of disappointment in defeat, made it simultaneously the opening speech of his next battle. Like John F. Kennedy's graceful concession to Senator Estes Kefauver after his defeat for the vice presidential nomination in 1956, Reagan's speech and demeanor may have served him over the longer term as well as or better than a victory.

Other farewells can only be farewells. As one might have anticipated, Reagan had a rather dramatic exit from the White House in 1989. He had been able, beating the historical odds, to give a powerful assist to the efforts of his own vice president, George Bush, to succeed him in the top post. As Bush's inauguration approached, he gave a major speech to the nation, laying out his view of his administration's accomplishments as well as the unfinished agenda he saw ahead.

Reagan understood that he should leave the stage to those coming after him. There was never a question in anyone's mind that he might remain in or near Washington, lingering uncomfortably as new management took over the company. Reagan would return home to California.

The actual departure scene, encompassing the breadth of Washington's monuments and institutions, was an evocative series of tableaux witnessed by millions on television. Following Bush's inaugural ceremony, the outgoing and incoming first couples walked together down the Capitol steps. The Reagans continued on, with the former president turning and saluting Bush, much as a military commander might transfer authority to a successor. Then they turned away, entering the waiting helicopter. Following a farewell flight around the familiar monuments of the capital, Reagan's helicopter disappeared into the enveloping sky, headed toward Andrews Air Force Base. Upon landing, completing the ritual, Reagan and a group of family, friends, staff, and journalists flew to California for a last time on the plane that had been Air Force One.

Reagan had often said that he would return to his long-time role as an after-dinner speaker. In that capacity, he would work to advance issues of particular importance, such as constitutional amendments requiring a balanced federal budget or allowing presidents to seek more than two terms. His speech to the Republican National Convention at Houston in 1992 showcased his optimistic, inclusive vision, delivered with care and conviction. The positive reaction, both in the convention hall and among the general public, was a reminder of the continuing hold of the leader and his vision on the American people.

Although no one could have known it at the time, the Houston speech became a farewell to his party and his country. On November 5, 1994, in a handwritten letter to the American people, President Reagan disclosed that he had been diagnosed with Alzheimer's disease—the same disease that inflicted "years of torment" on his mother. He wrote:

> Unfortunately, as Alzheimer's Disease progresses, the family often bears a heavy burden. I only wish there was some way I could spare Nancy from this painful experience. When the time comes, I am confident that with your help she will face it with faith and courage.
>
> In closing, let me thank you, the American people, for giving me the great honor of allowing me to serve as your President. When the Lord calls me home, whenever that may be, I will leave with the greatest love for this country of ours and eternal optimism for its future.
>
> I now begin the journey that will lead me into the sunset of my life. I know that for America there will always be a bright dawn ahead.

REAGAN ON LEADERSHIP: COMING, GOING, AND TIMING

- Timing is of critical importance to a leader. An action taken too soon or too late may have entirely different consequences than a decision made and implemented at the right time.

- Keep a clock in your own head when making key decisions. Deciding whether a course of action is a success or failure may depend in large part on the time frame for evaluation.

- Remember that people's attention is focused most strongly when a new leader assumes authority. Like Reagan, plan the rituals of transfer with care and use the early days to move rapidly on priorities, sending key signals both inside and outside your organization.

- Prepare for initial decisions before taking the reins. Do not wait and lose valuable time in the first days studying or considering courses of action—be fully prepared to implement your plans on day one.

- Remember that a farewell well handled—particularly in the context of a disappointment or defeat—may also become the basis for a new undertaking.

- Know when it's time to leave the stage. At the higher levels of leadership, especially when your organization is at a high point, others may see little need for change. Rely on the clock inside your head, and leave while your audience would rather have you stay.

PART 2

MANAGEMENT

———◆◆◆———

There is no limit to what a man can do or where
he can go if he doesn't mind who gets the credit.
—FROM PLAQUE ON PRESIDENT REAGAN'S
DESK IN OVAL OFFICE

CHAPTER 7

REAGAN'S MANAGEMENT APPROACH

———— ◆◆◆ ————

Much has been said about my management style, a style that's worked
successfully for me during eight years as governor of California and
for most of my presidency. The way I work is to identify the problem,
find the right individuals to do the job, and then let them go to it.
I've found this invariably brings out the best in people. They seem to
rise to their full capacity, and in the long run you get more done.
—RONALD REAGAN, 1987

THUS FAR, we have focused on those aspects of Reagan's leadership that most clearly define him as a leader in the public mind. Nonetheless, Reagan's leadership skills—his ability to conceive and communicate a compelling vision, his decisiveness, negotiating ability, and the rest—would have limited value unless they were harnessed to a coherent, consistent, and predictable management approach. It is through management that the leader's individual efforts can be dramatically magnified by the creativity, energy, and drive of the others who make up an organization. Far from being separate from leadership, management is an indispensable component of it.

Warren Bennis and Burt Nanus make a useful distinction between the leader and the manager:

> By focusing attention on a vision, the leader operates on the *emotional and spiritual resources* of the organization, on its values, commitment, and aspirations. The manager, by contrast, operates on the *physical resources* of the organization, on its capital, human skills, raw materials, and technology. Any competent manager can make it possible for people in the organization to earn a living. An excellent manager can see to it that work is done productively and efficiently, on schedule, and with a high level of quality. It remains for the effective leader, however, to help people in the organization know pride and satisfaction in their work. Great leaders often inspire their followers to high levels of achievement by showing them how their work contributes to worthwhile ends.

Not only do the manager and leader rely on one another; often a single person must exercise both skills. It is quite common for the head of a division in an enterprise to simultaneously exercise leadership and management functions. Many individuals who ascend to leadership positions do so because they have excelled in management; one factor in whether they succeed is their understanding of the additional requirements of their new role.

Ronald Reagan understood that management was critical to his effectiveness as a leader. Serving as chief executive in Sacramento and later in Washington, he succeeded because of his ability to bring the two sets of skills together. Indeed, he is unique among presidents in that management style, and its relation to his leadership, was an issue in his election. Following the widely known and generally criticized tendency of his predecessor to "micromanage"—reputedly down to the schedule of the White House tennis court—Reagan presented a "big picture" approach to the top job.

VISION-BASED MANAGEMENT

Reagan's management approach was consistent with his vision of leadership, in that both were ultimately based on empowering others:

> I don't believe a chief executive should supervise every detail of what goes on in his organization. The chief executive should set broad policy and general ground rules, tell people what he or she wants them to do, then let them do it; he should make himself (or *herself*) available, so that the members of his team can come to him if there is a problem. If there is, you can work together and, if necessary, fine-tune the policies. But I don't think a chief executive should peer constantly over the shoulders of the people who are in charge of a project and tell them every few minutes what to do.

As we saw in Chapter One, Reagan laid out what he called the "broad policy" with unmistakable clarity. Reagan's vision-based leadership style made possible a vision-based management approach. Bennis and Nanus discussed the power of a compelling vision inside an operating organization:

> A shared vision of the future also suggests measures of effectiveness for the organization and for all its parts. It helps individuals distinguish between what's good and what's bad for the organization, and what it's worthwhile to want to achieve. And most important, it makes it possible to distribute decision making widely. People can make difficult decisions without having to appeal to higher levels in the organization each time because they know what end results are desired. Thus, in a very real sense, individual behavior can be shaped, directed, and coordinated by a shared and empowering vision of the future.

Some might assume that having a chief executive focus on vision would mean less direction for staff than a micromanaging style. At least in large organizations, the opposite is more likely true. Certainly in the presidency, Reagan—the "big picture" man—gave clear direction, whereas Carter, the micromanager, left his organization adrift. Peggy Noonan, a lyrical writer credited with assisting Reagan in some of his most important speeches, quoted the observations of a colleague: "The idea of Reagan ruled. Everybody around him had a good idea of who he was and what he would do. He'd been in public life for twenty years, they knew what he stood for." As another veteran of the Reagan administration put it: "Every day when I got up and went to work, I knew what I had to do." By comparison, Bennis and Nanus quote an official from the previous administration who, though supportive of President Carter, could never divine what he stood for: "Working for him was like looking at the wrong side of a tapestry—blurry and indistinct."

PERSONNEL IS JOB ONE

As powerful as Reagan's vision was, he knew it was by no means self-implementing. To make a practical difference, he needed to obtain the agreement and support of the implementing executive bureaucracy. Bennis and Nanus quote John Young, former head of Hewlett-Packard, who observed: "Successful companies have a consensus from top to bottom on a set of overall goals. The most brilliant management strategy will fail if that consensus is missing."

For a president to forge such a working consensus is a daunting project. The chief executive of a public-sector organization can only look with longing at the tools commanded by his counterpart in the private sector—hiring, firing, and promotional authority; the discipline of the bottom line of profit and loss; a relatively circumscribed set of constituents to whom he must respond.

In contrast, a president of the United States has direct appointing authority over several thousand positions in an organization with millions of employees. Though the president, as chief executive, is legally accountable for the conduct of the bureaucracy, people in the permanent bureaucracy—there long before he arrived, there long after he goes—also have obligations to others. The ability of his appointees to effect change is limited by organizational inertia, Byzantine civil service rules, and the absence of shared assumptions as to what constitutes success. What is more, since Reagan sought to change the direction of government and challenged some of its long-held operating premises, additional resistance from inside as well as out was unavoidable. An operating consensus along the lines urged by Young for the private sector was not a realistic goal.

Nonetheless, Reagan made the best use of the tools at his command. On the strength of his vision and the resulting commitments he had made in numerous policy areas over years in public life, he was able to screen his personnel appointments on the basis of loyalty and support for his program. As we have previously seen, he broke precedent and began the process of recruitment prior to his election.

To succeed in *decentralizing* decision making and empowering personnel to most effectively achieve his vision, Reagan had to begin with a highly *centralized,* personally directed selection process. Early in his first term, when most key appointments were made, he dedicated two hours per week to review of appointments. What is more, the involvement of his office ran the gamut from direct "presidential appointments" (such as members of the judiciary or the cabinet and subcabinet, who also require U.S. Senate approval) to many lesser appointments traditionally left largely to the discretion of the cabinet secretaries. This style was the virtual opposite of the Carter administration's, which generally left the lesser appointments in the hands of the cabinet secretaries. Reagan's early and direct intervention in personnel selection not only empowered his administration with the energy of people who shared his vision; it also spared him a great amount of otherwise wasted time and energy that might have been lost in unproductive internecine battles over issues on which Reagan had expressed public positions. In contrast, the Carter administration's early lack of attention to personnel selection led to acrimony and dissension within various operating departments. The resulting managerial turmoil could not be cured even by continued, direct, distracting, and often public intervention by White House staff.

While personnel selection could launch the administration on a strong start, Reagan recognized that maintaining the energetic support of even the most committed appointees would be a continuing task. His team understood that his appointees, from the cabinet on down, would come under countervailing if not overwhelming pressures to protect the status quo. Among those applying the pressure: congressional committees, lobbying groups (sometimes including litigating arms), the news media—and the ubiquitous permanent Washingtonians, older and allegedly wiser heads who were always around to remind the newcomers how little difference they would make no matter how hard they tried!

Reagan had dealt with similar challenges, albeit on a smaller scale, as governor of California. In Sacramento he frequently convened his cabinet (along with top personal staff), sometimes as often as three or four times in a single week. Often they met in informal lunches on Mondays, preparing the governor for regularly scheduled Tuesday press conferences. These practices provided Reagan with informal as well as formal information exchanges, and they kept top appointees informed of the chief executive's most recent thoughts. When a decision came directly from the governor to his cabinet secretaries, rather than through his personal staff, Reagan felt it had much greater effect. Also important, such contact could boost the morale of appointees facing challenges in their own bailiwicks.

In the White House, Reagan modified his practices, reflecting the magnitude of the national government. At the recommendation of Edwin Meese, an expert in public management who had served as his chief of staff in Sacramento, Reagan established a "cabinet council" system. The work of the administration was divided into a small number of crosscutting issues: economic affairs, national security, legal policy, and so on. The councils were theoretically chaired by the president, though their meetings were generally led by a designated member of the cabinet. These councils provided a mechanism for the president's vision and prior commitments to be translated into departmental action. Symbolically and literally, they served to remind appointees that policies—and their consequences—were ultimately the province of the White House and the elected chief executive. Combined with the power that gravitated to the White House Office of Management and Budget because of increasing deficit spending and the resulting measures to rein in agency prerogative, the executive office assembled information that otherwise would have remained dispersed across the administration. This allowed the White House to hold department heads accountable for meeting specified results in areas critical to Reagan's vision—such as cutting regulations and limiting the growth of domestic discretionary spending programs (that is, those not classified as politically sacrosanct entitlements).

The administration also sought to maintain esprit de corps through annual meetings of all appointees, called "executive forums." On a regular basis the White House staff circulated copies of recent Reagan speeches and actions. For the idea of Reagan to rule, ongoing reinforcement was needed.

DIRECTION WITHOUT ORDERS

Reagan's success in communicating his vision, combined with his approach to delegation, meant that he rarely gave direct orders. As will be discussed in more detail in Chapter Nine, this style has significant advantages for the leader of a large organization, largely resulting from empowering others to act in behalf of the broader vision.

Some of his team found this disconcerting. Reagan's first secretary of state Alexander Haig, for example, sought explicit lines of authority—which would have the practical effect, whether intended or not, of limiting the options of the chief executive. Donald Regan, who served as Reagan's secretary of the treasury and later as White House chief of staff, felt adrift in what he later called the "Guesswork Presidency." In his memoir he quotes a notebook entry from March 1981, his second month as secretary:

> To this day I have never had so much as one minute alone with Ronald Reagan! Never has he, or anyone else, sat down in private to explain to me what is expected of me, what goals he would like to see me accomplish, what results he wants. Since I am accustomed to management by objective, where people have *in writing* what is expected, and explicit standards are set, this has been most disconcerting. How can one do a job if the job is not defined? I have been struggling to do what I consider the job to be, and let others tell me if I'm wrong, or not doing the right thing. (So far no one has said!) This . . . is dangerous.

Regan continued: "The President never told me what he believed or wanted to accomplish in the field of economics. I had to figure these things out like any other American, by studying his speeches and reading the newspapers."

The fact was that Regan could indeed figure out what Reagan wanted from those sources. As Edwin Meese points out, while Regan sought more direction from the chief executive, he handled his job as treasury secretary in line with Reagan's wishes. This result demonstrates the effectiveness of Reagan's communication of his vision and priorities, as well as an appropriate division of labor between the two men.

On the other hand, had Regan not performed in accordance with the president's wishes, he would certainly have heard from Reagan's immediate staff, or even from Reagan himself if necessary.

BACKING UP STAFF

A vision-based management approach, empowering individuals throughout the organization, requires a high degree of trust between an executive and his staff. It has often been remarked that Reagan tended to ascribe his own trusting nature to others, and that he would assume people were trustworthy until their actions demonstrated otherwise. On the basis of trust, he reposed great authority in his top staff.

Reagan's unequivocal backing of the strong stance advocated by Transportation Secretary Drew Lewis in the PATCO strike put people inside and outside the administration on notice that the chief executive would back up subordinates under challenge. Equally important, he backed up top staff when they were under fire. At various times he stood by people despite intense media and public pressure, and Attorney General Meese, Secretary of Labor Donovan, and Environmental Protection Agency Administrator Gorsuch—to name a few—benefited from his defense.

On the other hand, sometimes Reagan arguably backed up the wrong staff, at some cost. In the 1980 campaign, for example, he acquiesced in the wishes of his then-manager, John Sears, culminating in the departure of longtime aide

Michael Deaver. In effect, Sears had raised questions about Deaver's loyalty if not veracity, leading him to resign. Although Deaver eventually returned to Reagan's service after Sears himself was fired by Reagan, some have speculated quite reasonably that the previous closeness of the relationship was never fully restored. Reagan's backing of Sears's decisions can be understood as a matter of sound management practice, insofar as he had delegated authority to Sears. Nonetheless, the competing priority of backing up a trusted and invaluable staffer should probably have received greater attention.

It is also true that Reagan's backing up of staff could shade into an unwillingness to take action when objectively necessary. Reagan's distaste for personal confrontation was palpable. Like some other leaders whose orders could move armies into battle—Winston Churchill comes to mind—he had an aversion to interpersonal conflict. Although on some occasions, such as the firing of John Sears, he personally acted when required, in others, as with Donald Regan, he probably waited far too long. Executives would be well advised to follow Reagan at his best in this regard.

THE IRAN-CONTRA AFFAIR: THE GREAT EXCEPTION

For most of his two terms as president—and to the surprise of many—Reagan was widely viewed as an outstanding executive. While his techniques were not always conventional, the striking results he achieved gave even his critics pause. Perhaps the high point of his reputation in this regard came in September 1986, when *Fortune* magazine put him on its cover: "What Managers Can Learn from Manager Reagan."

Shortly thereafter, as if fate were waiting in the wings, the Iran-Contra scandal broke open. In his claims of not having taken part in illegal or unethical conduct, Reagan repeatedly professed his complete ignorance of what eventually came to light: a covert operations arm of the executive branch, working out of the White House complex itself. As Richard Neustadt later wrote, "Save for [Iran-Contra], our business schools and others might now be extolling Reagan's clean desk management, and its mythology might have bedeviled presidential studies for years to come."

The Iran-Contra affair doubtless reflected a breakdown in management. The question is whether the problem was in Reagan's management approach or its implementation.

It is not necessary to recapitulate the details of the Iran-Contra scandal to recognize that it could well have been avoided, had Reagan's management approach been faithfully applied.

Perhaps the main errors were in terms of personnel. At the beginning of his second term, Reagan was approached by his then–chief of staff, James Baker, and his treasury secretary, Regan, who together urged that they be allowed to switch jobs. Apparently relying on his complete trust in the judgment and motivations of the two individuals, he acquiesced. While Reagan's thought about the need to bring new blood into the administration in the second term may have had merit, it soon became clear that Donald Regan was unquestionably unsuited to his new position. Other dubious personnel decisions, at least in part a reflection on the unsuitability of the new chief of staff, followed. These ranged from the selection of the national security adviser to the de facto dismantling of the oversight capacity of the president's Foreign Intelligence Advisory Board. Putting to the side any question of Regan's legal culpability in the ensuing scandal, there is little question that others might have handled its denouement better.

Even the personnel problems might not have been fatal had not the entire operation been shrouded in secrecy. The foolish notions that underlay the scandal—arms for hostages, attempting to circumvent statutory requirements for foreign policy actions, a renegade operation located in the White House complex—would likely not have survived the normal give-and-take of meetings and decisions. It is likely they would have been smothered long before reaching Reagan's level. Had these notions somehow survived to the top, even had the president somehow viewed them favorably when presented together, there was an additional circuit breaker that might well have aborted the scheme. Nancy Reagan, the president's wife, routinely played a tremendously valuable role as a source of important information for her husband, particularly on personnel matters. Regrettably, secrecy foreclosed her involvement as well.

Nonetheless, Reagan was also blameworthy for not acting more rapidly in response to fast-moving events. After his initial error in endorsing the Baker-Regan switch, he compounded problems by not making rapid personnel changes. As George Will wrote in early 1987, "The lingering departure of Donald Regan in his own sweet time, more than three months late, is a debilitating result of the self-indulgence of a president who would rather not put himself through the unpleasantness of demonstrating that there are penalties for failure."

Will asked the right question of Reagan: "Do you want to be President?" Early in his second term—a time of peril for many presidents—Reagan seemed perilously disengaged from governance. A rogue secret operation might have started under any management system, but it metastasized dangerously when management was temporarily on holiday. Had Reagan followed his own management prescriptions as outlined in this section, the Iran-Contra scandal might have been avoided, or certainly need not have reached such a serious level. In the end, as discussed in Chapter Five, this leader—then 76 years of age—pulled himself and his administration back together, teaching a lesson in how to recover from failure. A critical part of the recovery was Reagan's reestablishment of strong management built on outstanding personnel choices.

FROM MANAGEMENT APPROACH TO MANAGEMENT RESULTS

Reagan's approach to management was an adjunct to his compelling vision. He understood that an organization was best managed by empowering others to implement the shared vision; the chief executive would not be doing his own job if he spent too much time peering over the shoulders of others. To obtain the organizational consensus that would allow such empowerment, Reagan initially centralized personnel selection to an unprecedented extent. He also moved certain issues that cut across the executive branch departments—the definition of which arose from his vision—directly into the White House for consideration and resolution. Simultaneously, he strengthened his ability to define success and ensure results in a time of growing deficit spending by using the Office of Management and Budget to enforce spending and regulatory priorities.

The succeeding chapters of this section will examine several critical elements of Reagan's management approach in greater detail. We will consider his use of priorities as a tool to ensure maximum concentration on the issues he judged most important to achieve his vision. We will then turn to his approach to delegation of authority. Finally, we will look at how Reagan used meetings—a key day-to-day tool that can make or break the effectiveness of executives and their organizations.

Flowing from its reliance on vision and empowering personnel, Reagan's management approach was implemented successfully—with extraordinary results—when its principles were followed. The role of the chief executive is indispensable. The signal achievements of Reagan's management approach, as well as the meltdown of the Iran-Contra scandal, can be traced back to Reagan himself.

REAGAN ON LEADERSHIP: REAGAN'S MANAGEMENT APPROACH

- Leadership, if it is to be actualized through results, must encompass a strong management approach.

- As an executive—especially a chief executive—you must combine leadership skills (relating to the emotional and spiritual needs of your organization) with managerial skills (relating to physical resources).

- If, as an executive, your leadership vision and management approach are consistent, they can come together as a powerful force. Reagan's consistent application of his belief in empowering individuals is a useful example.

- On the foundation of a compelling vision, you can empower your organization through Reagan's approach: The chief executive sets broad policy, tells people what is expected, and then lets them apply their own ingenuity without unnecessary interference.

- To the extent that your management approach relies on empowerment of staff and decentralization of authority, you must put correspondingly greater personal emphasis on initial personnel selection. Personnel should share your organization's vision and continually receive information and training that bolsters their commitment and updates their knowledge.

- A readily communicated and expansive vision, constantly communicated to staff, can empower the executive by providing direction without orders.

- Back up your staff—but do not let your general support of staff allow you to rationalize a reluctance to take timely, decisive personnel actions.

- In analyzing a management breakdown, distinguish between problems in the management approach and problems in its implementation.

CHAPTER 8

FIRST THINGS FIRST

———◆———

If there is any one "secret" of effectiveness, it is concentration. Effective executives do first things first and they do one thing at a time.
—PETER F. DRUCKER

ONE OF THE most important challenges facing every leader is how to set priorities for his own time and effort, as well as the organization he leads. Peter Drucker describes the problem:

> There are always more important contributions to be made than there is time available to make them. Any analysis of executive contributions comes up with an embarrassing richness of important tasks; any analysis of executives' time discloses an embarrassing scarcity of time available for the work that really contributes. No matter how well an executive manages his time, the greater part of it will still not be his own.

There is a pressing need to set priorities, to determine what parts of a leader's vision will receive attention over other matters.

When Reagan became governor of California, his executive experience was limited to heading the Screen Actors Guild. After two successful terms in the state capitol of the nation's most populous state, he assumed the presidency with proven management experience and skill. Shortly before the 1980 election, referring to President Jimmy Carter, Reagan told Martin Anderson, "The problem with Carter is that he tries to do everything at once and he tries to do too much of it himself. If we win we are going to set priorities and do things one at a time."

Their differing approaches collided in a meeting between the incoming and outgoing presidents shortly after the election. In his memoirs, Carter explained, "I considered this visit very important, and had carefully prepared a list of the *most significant issues* that needed to be discussed—issues which only a President could ultimately resolve."

In Carter's view, many issues required personal presidential attention. All told, Carter shared his thoughts on "fifteen to twenty subjects" in less than an hour. After outlining some key points on management of nuclear attack against the United States, he discussed "some top-secret agreements with other nations." Carter continued:

> I then talked to him about China, describing the careful balance that had been worked out by Presidents Nixon and Ford and myself and emphasizing the sensitivity of the Chinese to the Taiwan issue. I reviewed such defense considerations as the interrelationship among cruise missiles, the "stealth" aircraft, and the B-1 bomber. Then I listed some the advantages to our country of honoring the terms of SALT II, pending its ratification, and of maintaining a strong proliferation policy. [Reagan] sat quietly through a brief review of the latest developments in Afghanistan and the hostage situation.
>
> I told him how difficult it was for any President to get Congress to approve adequate foreign-aid legislation. . . . I outlined my plans for completing a solid budget, and reminded him about my long-standing freeze on the hiring of federal employees.

Finally, I covered some special presidential problems with regard to the Germans and a few other European countries concerning defense matters; Poland; Nicaragua; the proposed F-15 sales to Saudi Arabia; and the need for aggressive action by our leaders in the Middle East peace process. This list comprised *some of the essential items* that needed to be discussed personally by the two of us.

In recounting the meeting in his memoirs, Carter expressed disappointment in Reagan's reaction: "He waited patiently until I had finished, and then the President-elect asked me to conduct all foreign and defense business with his adviser, Richard Allen, pending his choice of a Secretary of State, a Secretary of Defense, and other members of his Cabinet." The outgoing president concluded: "It had been a pleasant visit, but I was not sure how much we had accomplished."

Perhaps reflecting his experience in the movie industry— with its tight time schedules, tough directors and producers, and unremitting attention to the bottom line—Reagan's focus was on results. He understood that a leader must work within the discipline of priorities if success is to be clearly defined and then achieved. As Drucker observed, when executives set clear priorities and are relentless in doing things one at a time, they are able to accomplish more—and in less time—than others. He added, "The people who get nothing done often work a great deal harder."

Reagan's two top priorities flowed directly from his vision: cut taxes and regulations; strengthen defense and reestablish the U.S. military posture vis-à-vis the U.S.S.R. At the outset of his administration—beginning on the first day—Reagan made economic recovery his number one action item. Simultaneously he unleashed the unprecedented peacetime buildup in armaments that would later enable him to negotiate from strength, achieving unprecedented nuclear arms reduction with the Soviet Union. As Martin Anderson explained:

Remember that Ronald Reagan had spent ten or fifteen years developing and honing his message, and he locked it in during the campaign. As a result, when we took over the White House in January 1981 there was not a hell of a lot of *new* policy for us to develop. Reagan had already done it. . . . It wasn't going to be a supermarket of things to choose from like it was under Jimmy Carter.

Ronald Reagan knew what he wanted to do. From the outset he set the priorities which everyone knew: national security and economic growth, and in the first eighteen months, 90 percent of our efforts were on economic growth.

Though Reagan himself tended to refer to both top priorities interchangeably, as if they were on a single track, the fact was that his economic program received the greatest initial attention. This was of course consistent with his military buildup—obviously a strong economy was the basis for the United States' ultimate advantage in the defense escalation. Further, there was no conflict between his priorities insofar as the most significant acts in the initial months vis-à-vis the Soviet Union were rhetorical (changing the perceptions of the relationship) and preparatory (building up arms to bargain them away).

It is important to recognize, at the same time, that a chief executive also has additional commitments that reflect the highest priorities of one or more constituencies inside and outside the organization. The extent to which he wishes to expressly define his view of the interrelationship among his priorities is a decision to be considered carefully in light of how the top priority is to be achieved. For example, Reagan was strongly supported by "social conservatives" whose greatest goals included legal limitations on abortion and other highly controversial matters. He tended to look for areas of common ground where such groups might support his top priorities, exemplified in his famous speech before the National

Association of Evangelicals in March 1983, where he characterized the Soviet Union as the "Evil Empire." While he publicly endorsed many of their more controversial stands, he did not press them to an extent that would ultimately threaten public support for his own top priorities.

Similarly, leaving some degree of uncertainty among opponents or competitors as to the interrelationship among priorities can be useful in achieving the top priorities. If each priority is going to be opposed, having several moving simultaneously or launching them one after another might make it more likely that the most favored priority at a given time is achieved. This would be consistent with Reagan's approach as a negotiator, as well as his use of the indirect approach.

Reagan communicated his overarching priorities so effectively that nearly 70 percent of the American people were reported able to name at least one. This compared to ratings from 15 percent to 45 percent in the preceding Johnson, Nixon, Ford, and Carter administrations.

The administration, of course, had policy positions and interests in a broad range of other matters. But management decisions—from personnel selection to budget to communications—were remarkably reflective of the top priorities. There is little question that this discipline was effective.

It is important to note that there were costs to this approach as well. An approach of "first things first" may run risks if it also means, as a practical matter, "second things not at all." In focusing so intently on the top priorities, other areas were viewed not on their own terms, but largely as they related to the top priorities. As a result, foreseeably unsuitable initial personnel choices in low-priority areas—including environmental protection, housing, and labor—led to lost opportunities and even scandals. Famously, in public settings Reagan even forgot the names of several of his top appointees in those areas (which, on the other hand, did allow him the benefit of the doubt of some distance from them). Such problems, if not contained, might have threatened the administration's ability to achieve its top priorities, but in Reagan's case they did not.

Nonetheless, leaders looking to Reagan's example here may wish to put in place management mechanisms to ensure that nonpriority items do not fall below a minimum of competent administration. Such mechanisms, made part of the responsibility of top staff, need not take significant time on the part of the chief executive. In fact, it is possible that such an approach might have taken less of Reagan's time than he ultimately spent in personally dealing with the problems arising from scandals and personnel problems in low-priority areas.

Those problems, real as they were, nonetheless pale in comparison to the consequences of not setting—and enforcing—top priorities. If a leader simply responds to the random demands placed by others, he is allowing others to set his priorities. At the helm of a corporation with multiple constituencies—the public, the press and opinion leaders, competitors and allies, employees, the investment community, government regulators of various types—this is a critical challenge. In the American presidency, the challenge is magnified and the time frame compressed. What is more, every member of the organization, even if well versed in the leader's overall vision, needs to understand the priorities clearly enough to meet the same tests within their own more limited but no less important domains.

Ultimately, executives operating without the compass of priorities will not be performing their jobs at all. Drucker explains:

In particular, a top group which lets itself be controlled by the pressures will slight the one job no one else can do. It will not pay attention to the outside of the organization. It will therefore lose touch with the only reality, the only area in which there are results. For the pressures always favor what goes on inside. They always favor what has happened over the future, the crisis over the opportunity, the immediate and visible over the real, and the urgent over the relevant.

While adherence to priorities makes it possible for the executive leadership to do the job "no one else can do," it does not ensure it. Setting priorities determines the proper subject matter of the work, but delegation—the distribution of responsibility by the executive in charge—ensures that each person adds the most value to the task at hand.

REAGAN ON LEADERSHIP: FIRST THINGS FIRST

- Your organization's top priorities should flow clearly, directly, and inevitably from the leader's vision.

- You need a small number of top priorities; if you have a dozen "top" priorities you have none.

- Your top priorities should inform every area of management over which you have influence or responsibility—from personnel to budget to communication.

- As chief executive, you should focus on implementing your top priorities, one at a time.

- How to communicate the intended interrelationship among several top priorities is a separate decision to be considered in the context of best achieving your goals.

- If you do not set priorities, others will set them for you as they seek to meet their own priorities, or your organization may be driven by the force of random events.

- As an executive, when you focus on priorities you necessarily maintain your own attention to the world outside of your organization—and the need for concrete results to be achieved by specific dates.

- Remember that while the setting of priorities is critical to your success and that of your organization, it should be combined with an approach to delegation of authority that ensures the best use of each individual's talents.

CHAPTER 9

DO ONLY WHAT
YOUR SUBORDINATES
CANNOT DO

———— ✦ ————

He had no vain conceit of being himself all;
and did those things which only he could do.
—SAMUEL TAYLOR COLERIDGE,
WRITING OF GEORGE WASHINGTON

WHEN AN EXECUTIVE sets *priorities,* he focuses the attention of his organization on those tasks he judges essential to achievement of his vision. Through *delegation* of tasks and responsibilities within the organization he ensures that each person adds maximum value toward meeting the priorities.

Everyone aspiring to management responsibility must give considerable thought to delegation. Inexperienced managers frequently make misjudgments in this regard. Some do not delegate enough. Where individuals are promoted to management as a result of excelling at staff work, they may have difficulty shifting their focus from their own productivity to enabling others to add value. Highly trained individuals such as doctors and lawyers and scientists may also overestimate the significance of their own skills and expertise while underestimating the actual or potential contributions of others. A related mistake of many new managers is to give too much personal attention to the area of work from which they have risen, detracting from their effectiveness in their new role.

Another group of managers delegates too broadly, allowing staff to assume, by design or inadvertence, management prerogatives. Especially at high levels in an organization, this can pose serious problems. The staff may not have access to the complete information available to the manager—or, if they do, they may nonetheless lack the perspective that comes from accountability for the consequences of a misjudgment.

If everyone talks about delegation and the need to do it better, why is so much of the discussion so often in vain? Peter Drucker explains: "The reason why no one listens is simple: As usually presented, delegation makes little sense. If it means that somebody else ought to do part of '*my* work,' it is wrong. One is paid for doing one's own work. And if it implies, as the usual sermon does, that the laziest manager is the best manager, it is not only nonsense, it is immoral."

Drucker found that whenever a harried executive analyzed his calendar, he would inevitably find that "there just is not time enough to do the things the executive himself considers important, himself wants to do, and is himself committed to doing. The only way he can get to the important things is by pushing on others anything that can be done by them at all."

The best approach to delegation has been suggested by observers ranging from Coleridge, an English poet and literary critic at the turn of the 19th century, to Drucker, a revered management guru today. The rule for effective delegation— useful for a chief executive evaluating any proposed use of his time or authority—is:

If anyone else can perform a task as well as or better than I could do it, then I should not do it.

By strictly adhering to this rule an executive can reliably gain maximum value from his team. Any time that a manager performs a task that could be handled by his staff, he is taking time away from tasks that only he could perform. At the same time, he is not getting the best performance from the staff. For optimal results, this rule should be applied at every level in an organization.

THE IMPORTANCE OF EMPOWERING SUBORDINATES

Ronald Reagan instinctively understood this rule and applied it flawlessly. In part because of his own public jokes about his relaxed work habits and his consciously calm demeanor in the face of the legendary burdens of the modern presidency, Reagan the manager is sometimes dismissed as someone who simply "got others to do all the work." The quotation from Coleridge that serves as the epigraph for this chapter is cited with some wryness, if not condescension, by Reagan chronicler Lou Cannon, who added,

> Reagan was no Washington, but he had even less conceit and was similarly convinced of the wisdom of doing only those things that could not be done for him by someone else. The paradox of the Reagan presidency was that it depended totally upon Reagan for ideological inspiration while he depended totally upon others for all aspects of governance except his core ideas and powerful performances. . . . He left to others what he called the "details" of government, a category that included the preparation of a budget, the formulation of foreign policy, the translation of ideas into legislative proposals and the resolution of conflicts among his principal advisers.

While Reagan was a man of many paradoxes, his manner of delegation should not be counted among them. His approach was immensely effective at several levels.

Delegation, as stated earlier, is simply the way in which the manager gets the best from all the personnel entrusted to him—including himself. Reagan understood that others could in fact handle the day-to-day personnel actions, the preparation of the budget, the legislative drafting, and so on. His value-added role related to strategy, communication, and high-level decisions. This approach is also seen in other familiar organizational settings. For example, a middle-aged football coach may have much less ability to play quarterback or guard than a strapping youth, while undoubtedly being the best qualified to coach. Perhaps because of his background as a professional actor—another enterprise based on performance of a team where each individual has a clearly defined role, orchestrated on a rapid time frame toward a precise result—Reagan did not share the need of some executives (famously including some recent U.S. presidents) to appear able to perform every task in his organization. His approach reflected the realization that when a manager routinely takes on the details despite the fact that others could handle them as well or better, he may not be acting in the best interest of the organization.

A vanity-related weakness afflicting some managers is the need to be surrounded by people whose attributes are nearly identical to their own, or who manifestly possess less ability in relevant areas. Reagan was generally assisted by individuals of great and recognized ability whose skills complemented his own. To the surprise of some long-time supporters, he selected James Baker as his first presidential chief of staff. He recognized that the value of bringing the Texan's managerial and political skills into the team far outweighed any qualms arising from his prior service in opposing political campaigns.

Later, as part of his recovery from the Iran-Contra affair, Reagan turned to former senator Howard Baker for the same task, in no way threatened by the fact that many considered Baker to be as well prepared for the presidency as Reagan himself. In the same vein, he reached out to persons of recognized stature for other key positions, including Secretary of State Shultz, Defense Secretary Weinberger, and numerous others.

THE ECONOMY OF EXECUTIVE DECISION MAKING

Most chief executives have significant leeway—often more than they initially imagine—in defining their direct role in implementing decisions. As one example of particular relevance here because of Reagan's management approach, consider personnel actions. There is little reason why virtually any personnel action should be implemented by the chief executive. He should retain the option to make the final decision on hiring and firing, promoting or demoting, above a certain administrative level. But generally, with respect to all except those reporting directly to the chief executive, personnel actions can be taken by a chief of staff or another empowered in a similar way. Even where the chief executive has made the decision, whether to present the action as *his* decision should itself be recognized as a decision of some consequence.

This reflects what might be called the economy of executive decision making. Every decision visibly, directly taken by the chief executive has a cost. The cost might be public controversy; it might be the goodwill of one or more groups or individuals; it might be nothing more than the time needed to explain the rationale. This is true not only in the case of personnel issues, but across the range of managerial choice. For an organization to obtain the greatest value from the chief executive, and successively from each management level below, decisions should generally be carried out at the lowest appropriate level.

There are situations, to be sure, where the executive's personal role in a decision may be usefully communicated to make a broader point about the organization's priorities. One such example arose when a Reagan nominee for high legal office was revealed to have used illicit drugs in compromising circumstances earlier in his adult life. Signals strongly suggesting that the nominee withdraw emanated unmistakably from the White House itself. Otherwise, decisions that need not have been made by the executive—or need not have been communicated as made personally by the chief executive—may occasion activity that does not add value toward accomplishing the priorities of the enterprise.

Equally important, empowering subordinates empowers the executive. Where others inside and outside the enterprise understand that subordinates have authority to speak for their manager, it multiplies his influence. Many decisions otherwise apparently too small to justify the executive's direct attention, much less his open intervention, might be handled efficiently in this way, advancing the organization's priorities.

When others recognize that subordinates are empowered to speak for the leader, but there is some uncertainty about the leader's direct involvement in a given issue, the leader's tactical flexibility can be preserved. In a negotiating context—and as we have seen, many interactions can be viewed as negotiations—this too can add significant value. As suggested in Chapter Three, this includes the option—rarely to be exercised—of overriding a subordinate's action while not jeopardizing trust among the various parties. This may be required on the basis of additional information or changed circumstances.

The distance delegation creates between the leader and the action can also be important in other ways. As previously noted, Reagan understood that a relatively unimportant action, because it is comprehensible in terms of everyday life, can take on tremendous symbolic significance with the public. It is for this reason that conventional politicians devote so much energy to uncovering an otherwise inconsequential fact that can be dramatized into a broader representation of an opponent. For example, when the American automobile industry was battered by competition from foreign imports in the 1980s, political leaders who drove foreign-made cars could be credibly characterized as lacking concern about the fate of American automobile workers—or even disloyal to the nation. Whether this should be considered an accurate indicator of such sentiments might be open to question. There is no question, though, that it did have resonance with the many families who understood that their own car purchasing decisions might have direct economic consequences for other families, perhaps in the same cities or neighborhoods.

In the same way, people who might otherwise have no basis to evaluate the economic policy of the United States might feel confident in drawing wide-ranging conclusions from a discrete decision—such as the fate of an old but small government program—known to be taken directly by a president. Or they might draw conclusions about his character from a public representation—which might or might not be accurate—by an employee whom the president personally disciplined or fired or otherwise had contact with.

Reagan, characteristically, did not publicly discuss this part of his management approach, though it was evident to one and all. Winston Churchill, equally characteristically, wrote about the same point from his own experience. As the First World War broke out in 1914, Churchill found that he enjoyed "enormous prestige" from his earlier preparations for a conflict that many others did not foresee. As a result, his own pride—vanity, perhaps—drew him "into taking minor military responsibilities upon my shoulders which exposed me to all those deadly risks on a small scale that await those in high stations who come too closely into contact with action in detail."

Churchill, then a member of the British War Cabinet, traveled to Belgium, where he became so involved in the fighting on the ground that he offered his resignation so that he might "see things through on the spot." He continued:

> Lucky indeed it was for me that my offer was not accepted, for I should only have been involved in the command of a situation which locally at any rate had already been rendered hopeless by the general course of the War. In all great business very large errors are excused and even unperceived, but in definite and local matters small mistakes are punished out of all proportion. I might well have lost all the esteem I gained by the mobilization and readiness of the fleet, through getting mixed up in the firing-lines at Antwerp. Those who are charged with the direction of supreme affairs must sit on the mountain-tops of control; they must never descend into the valleys of direct physical and personal action.

The perils of such recognized intervention into detail are multiplied where, as in Reagan's case, the executive is also a leader who embodies his vision. In such a case all the power the vision gains from the leader's identification with it can be turned against it with equal or greater force. For Reagan, being personally identified with such "small mistakes" might have posed a serious threat to public confidence in his economic policies, for example, during the bleak recessionary days of 1981 and 1982. Similarly, his rearmament policies might have lost public confidence.

Reagan combined publicly recognized personal empathy with managerial distance (including his practice of allowing subordinates to gain an unusual degree of public credit for their contributions). This led some observers to separate their views of Reagan the man—for whom they felt affection— from their reaction to the perceived results of his policies. Tip O'Neill, the late Democratic Speaker of the House of Representatives who was as reliably liberal as Reagan was conservative, wrote with some frustration:

> The public's double vision of Reagan was brought home to me one day by a construction worker who came to see me at my district office in Boston. He was a strong, husky fellow who had fallen off a roof and had suffered a spinal cord injury that meant he would never walk again. He was angry because the administration wanted to tax workman's compensation benefits, and he wanted to see if anything could be done.
>
> But while he was in, he decided to register another complaint: "Tip," he said, "I've voted for you all my life, but I think you're too tough on the president."
>
> I was stunned. "Who do you think is cutting your benefits?" I asked.
>
> "Not the president," he replied confidently. "He's got nothing to do with it. It's the people around him."

Even granting the literary license that one gifted Irish-American storyteller might have exercised in characterizing another, O'Neill's point was not inaccurate. In a similar vein, some Reagan backers, dismayed by his administration's unwillingness to give top priority to some policies for which the president had expressed public support, publicly asked his top appointees to "let Reagan be Reagan."

REAGAN'S "PASSIVE" MANAGEMENT STYLE

As a leader, Reagan was a strikingly effective advocate of major changes in American public policy. As a manager, many found it incongruous that the power of his vision allowed him to direct very large and complex organizations—the government of America's most populous state and the executive branch of the national government—with a minimum of direct orders. Many found it curious that this most persuasive and decisive leader achieved his ends through what has often been termed a "passive" management style.

Martin Anderson viewed this as "an eccentricity":

> So everyone overlooked and compensated for the fact that he made decisions like an ancient king or a Turkish pasha, passively letting his subjects serve him, selecting only those morsels of public policy that were especially tasty. Rarely did he ask searching questions or demand to know why someone had or had not done something. He just sat back in a supremely calm, relaxed manner and waited until important things were brought to him. And then he would act, quickly, decisively, and usually, very wisely.

Less charitably, Donald Regan, looking back on his service as chief of staff, recounted his 1985 presentation of "a formal paper recommending a course of action for the future." The document "focused on three critical objectives: maintenance of the economic recovery, foreign policy, and the legislative agenda." Regan assumed that his draft plan would serve as the basis for additional discussion, to be implemented through a series of presidential "marching orders" on an array of matters throughout the administration.

> Instead, Ronald Reagan read the paper while he was at the ranch and handed it back to me on his return without spoken or written comment.
>
> "What did you think of it?" I asked.
>
> "It's good, the President replied," nodding in approval. "It's really good, Don."
>
> I waited for him to say more. He did not. He had no questions to ask, no objections to raise, no instructions to issue.

I realized that the policy that would determine the course of the world's most powerful nation for the next two years and deeply influence the fate of the Republican party in the 1986 midterm elections had been adopted without amendment. It seemed, also, that I had been authorized as Chief of Staff to make the necessary arrangements to carry out the policy. It was taken for granted that the President would do whatever was asked of him to make the effort a success.

Reagan's reaction was in keeping with his management approach: "As long as they are doing what you have in mind, don't interfere, but if somebody drops the ball, intervene and make a change." To be sure, the president would respond if presented with a scenario he found wanting. If a subordinate rewrote a speech, for example, in a way that did not reflect his intent, Reagan might become visibly angry. He also resisted numerous staff entreaties to raise taxes to reduce the mounting budget deficit. But if a plan of action, a personnel decision, or other issue was presented in a manner he judged consistent with his vision, he tended to approve it with a minimum of comment or adjustment.

This approach, based in part on trust and his attention to personnel selection, kept the number of decisions requiring Reagan's personal imprimatur at a minimum. It also affixed accountability, to the maximal extent, with staff. It was a good fit for a vision-based organization in which both tactics and staff were ultimately expendable if necessary to achieve priorities. Reagan's combination of personal empathy and organizational toughness led Anderson to characterize him, memorably, as "a warmly ruthless man."

DOING WHAT ONLY THE LEADER CAN DO

One of the key benefits of skillful delegation is that it makes it possible for the chief executive to best serve his organization.

In this sense delegation might be viewed as a mechanism by which effective management makes effective leadership possible. As Drucker pointed out, the chief executive has quite specific responsibilities that no one else can take on; they cannot be delegated. Most important, he must constantly be in touch with the world outside the organization, making certain that results are being achieved. He must keep an eye fixed on the future. He must maintain and communicate the organization's vision, both inside and outside the organization. He must constantly be listening, learning, and updating priorities.

In terms of his own time and effort, Reagan gave precedence to his role as communicator of the administration's vision. He understood that his skills in presenting the vision and priorities of his administration fit well into the "bully pulpit," Theodore Roosevelt's apt and lasting description of the American presidency.

Communication, of course, is a two-way transaction. Reagan methodically maintained sources of outside information. This was important at several levels. It provided him with continuing understanding of the general scene from which he, like any chief executive, might otherwise become detached. Equally valuable, particularly for a chief executive with a penchant for delegation, he maintained a sense of outside views of the performance of his administration. He was a longtime reader—continuing into the presidency—of periodicals whose judgment helped inform his worldview, such as *National Review* and *Human Events*. He also set aside time to personally respond to many letters from members of the public. For a trusted few, the White House provided a special post office box meant to ensure the president's personal attention.

Another and often related executive attribute that can be made more likely by delegation is the ability to "think outside the box." Where an executive generally shares the work, education, and experience of his staff, or is submerged in daily detail, he might be less likely to make the unconventional associations that can result in conceptual breakthroughs. To the amazement (and sometimes consternation) of friends and foes alike, Reagan constantly asked basic questions that might lead to such breakthroughs. Perhaps the most important example is the development of the intercontinental ballistic missile defense system Reagan called the Strategic Defense Initiative. This resulted from his personal questioning of the premises of American nuclear strategy, apparently arising from a visit to the North American Aerospace Defense Command in 1979. Similarly, Reagan's personal judgment about the significance of Gorbachev's new leadership in the Soviet Union and the opportunity for nuclear arms reduction was decisive in his negotiating approach. It was not the result of a staff suggestion or a consensus among national opinion leaders.

Reagan's willingness to look at old issues in unconventional ways probably reflected his own unconventional background for political leadership; many questions long considered settled among experts were fresh for him. At the same time, his strong self-confidence permitted him to ask basic but telling questions that might have seemed self-evident or embarrassing to conventional politicians eager to exhibit their own knowledge. Anderson reports that President Reagan opened his first meeting with the imposing chairman of the Federal Reserve Board, establishment epitome Paul Volcker, with a question: "I was wondering if you could help me with a question that's often put to me. I've had several letters from people who raise the question of why we need any Federal Reserve at all. They seem to feel that it is the Fed that causes much of our monetary problems and that we would be better off if we abolished it. Why do we need the Federal Reserve?" Reagan's willingness to politely challenge one of the most powerful people in the world to justify his existence might not be a bad example for other executives to remember.

A chief executive necessarily stands alone in his ability to resolve policy disputes among competing parts of the organization he leads. Some of Reagan's top appointees expressed frustration that he would not intercede more predictably and often. One of his favored mechanisms in this regard, which fit his approach to leadership and management, was the production of presidential speeches. On matters ranging from economic reform to the Strategic Defense Initiative to arms control negotiation, the president would use the drafting process to draw out various perspectives, with his ultimate decisions reflected in a presidential address.

Reagan recognized that much of the added value of the chief executive's job comes from the application of his judgment. The staff presumably possesses knowledge and expertise far greater than that of the executive, which he can place in the service of his judgment. A chief executive should not become so immersed in minutiae, or so exhausted by bustle, that he cannot master breaking events with equanimity, dispatch, and resolve.

The most significant decisions—those that can only be made at the top—often do not arise separately and sequentially, like chapters in a book. They often come unbidden, in infelicitous platoons, at inopportune moments. Consider the autumn weekend that began on Friday, October 21, 1983. After traveling to Augusta, Georgia, Reagan was awakened at 4:00 A.M. Saturday for an emergency meeting on the developing crisis in Grenada. Later on Saturday his golf game was interrupted by a hostage incident near the course, which included several White House aides and engaged his direct involve-ment. On Sunday at 2:30 A.M. he was again awakened by staff, this time reporting the terrorist bombing of the marine barracks in Lebanon. Over the week that followed, he worked constantly to deal with the domestic and international ramifications of these crises, while also discharging ongoing duties. There can be little doubt that his sense of perspective and ability to take decisive action were bolstered by his approach to delegation.

Reagan's approach also enabled him to assume a unifying role, both inside and outside his administration. By maintaining his focus on vision and results and minimizing the number of decisions in which he personally intervened, he limited the costs that inevitably accrue from decision making over time. As Reagan left office in 1989, Robert J. Samuelson recognized this aspect of the president's style: "Eisenhower and Reagan shared a common characteristic disparaged by their critics: an ability to stay above events. . . . Like Eisenhower, Reagan sensed that a president cannot succeed unless he is a unifying figure. And he cannot be that if he becomes too deeply embroiled in too many political firefights."

REAGAN ON LEADERSHIP: DO ONLY WHAT YOUR SUBORDINATES CANNOT DO

- Effective delegation makes it possible for an organization to get maximum value from each individual.

- Remember the rule for executives: If anyone else can perform a task as well as or better than you could, then you should not do it.

- Your ability to delegate broadly depends on the quality of your personnel selections.

- The economy of decision making suggests that a chief executive's ability to perform his role can be increased by limiting the number of decisions requiring his personal direction or imprimatur. The organization can be best served where its vision and priorities are advanced by empowered employees who have received direction without orders.

- An executive who takes on too many small tasks risks having confidence in the organization's broader vision undermined by otherwise inconsequential events.

- Delegation can create the distance a chief executive needs to maintain tactical flexibility in the service of strategic resolve.

- Delegation is the mechanism by which management makes operational leadership possible. It allows the chief executive to focus attention on the things no one else in the organization can do. The executive's necessary roles include communicating with the outside world, maintaining a clear focus on results and a readiness for rapid decision, and serving as a unifying figure.

CHAPTER 10

MAKE MEETINGS USEFUL

———— ◆◆◆ ————

The meeting, the report, or the presentation are the typical work
situation of the executive. They are his specific, everyday tools.
—PETER F. DRUCKER

A TOP EXECUTIVE necessarily spends a large share of
his time in meetings. Some are intended to lead to decisions.
Others inform management of options or developments relating to issues of continuing concern. Sometimes they are intended to provide key staffers a means to become known to
top management. Some are used to obtain reassurance from
top executives that staff interpretation of a priority or directive is accurate and efficient—and to acquire authority for a
midcourse correction if not. Still others, particularly in very
large organizations, are held for symbolic reasons. For example, the president of the United States may meet with a group
of chief executive officers or Eagle Scouts or foreign digni-
taries to send broader signals about America, to exhibit the
nation's respect for specific individuals or accomplishments,
and so on.

In this television age most of us have seen Ronald Reagan
filmed in symbolic meetings and presentations. As might be
expected from a former professional actor, he handled

them with aplomb—whether opening a cabinet meeting at a critical juncture or offering all our heartfelt congratulations to triumphant American Olympic athletes. We will explore further, in the next section of the book, the highly developed communications skills that made such performances so effective.

DECISION-MAKING MEETINGS

In discussing how to make a meeting effective, Peter Drucker noted "the obvious but usually disregarded rule that one can either direct a meeting and listen for the important things being said, or one can take part and talk; one cannot do both. . . . The cardinal rule is to focus it from the start on contribution." In meetings intended to lead to decisions, such as cabinet meetings or meetings with top campaign staff, Reagan tended to listen rather than speak. However, when necessary to meet his ends, he would not hesitate to intervene directly.

In his memoirs, Reagan wrote about his general approach to leading meetings in the context of a spring 1981 discussion set to resolve his administration's internal division on the question of how to respond to the increasing flood of Japanese car imports. Prior to the meeting he had concluded that the best policy would be to side with those who opposed mandatory limitations on Japanese imports:

> I agreed with them but kept quiet. In Washington, I was following the same practice I had followed in Sacramento: I invited all the members of the cabinet to give their views on all sides of an issue (everything except the "political ramifications" of my decisions) and sometimes, as in this case, the result was a heated debate—and if I was leaning a certain way, I tried not to tip my advisors off, to ensure that I'd hear all sides.

Sometimes, as in this case, Reagan would himself propose a third way based on what he learned (in this case, "voluntary" reductions in exports by the Japanese, to head off congressional attempts to impose mandatory limitations).

Reagan liked to convene as broad a group as was manageable to assist him in making important decisions. This was the source of his heavy reliance on his cabinet in Sacramento, and his later efforts to preserve some semblance of that approach in Washington. Perhaps in part because he was himself the ultimate generalist, he tried to ensure that technical information was judged and put to use in a broader context:

> I told the cabinet members that I didn't want them to speak up only on the matters that affected their own departments. They were all my advisors, I said, and I wanted to hear everything each of them had to say about whatever topic we were considering, whether it involved their department or not, including any reservations they might have about a proposal; this gave me the opportunity to get opinions from a variety of perspectives, not only from the people who might be supporting a certain project or program.

Reagan was also willing to break protocol within meetings when doing so might bring in additional information or shift the balance of a discussion toward his preferred result. Martin Anderson has written about a White House cabinet meeting at which the attorney general proposed to limit illegal immigration by means of a national identity card. The notion was that employers would be alerted to citizenship status in a foolproof way, protecting them from liability for illegally hiring foreign nationals.

Strict rules of protocol govern cabinet meetings with a president. Each chair at the table is assigned to a specified cabinet secretary, based on the relative rank of the department represented. White House staff are allowed to attend as silent observers, generally sitting against the surrounding walls in armless chairs.

Following the presentation by the attorney general, Reagan asked if there were any comments. Perhaps the strength of the presentation made opposition seem futile. No cabinet members offered thoughts. Anderson raised his hand from the staff seats, aware that he was thereby "breaking an unwritten rule, the rule that says senior staff members may sit in on cabinet meetings but they are not to speak unless spoken to." Reagan recognized him to speak. Anderson made light of the identity card scheme—suggesting tattooing as a less expensive, more effective alternative—breaking a new conversational path that ended when Reagan himself administered the coup de grâce. The president's humorous but lethal quip: "Maybe we should just brand all the babies."

By remaining silent or participating in the give-and-take of such meetings while having top staffers such as Edwin Meese direct discussions, Reagan sought to best apply his own abilities in reaching a solution. He conferred a semblance of equality to the discussion, leaving his own views unclear or at least unstated in order to draw out the best from others. In other situations, particularly after he became president and there was a possibility of news leaks of his statements, he might maintain a discreet silence. But at the end of the day, Reagan would reassume the task that was his alone: "Everyone pitched in and was involved in the give-and-take of debate, but when the discussion was over, they all knew it was up to me and me alone to make the decision."

To get the most from such meetings, Reagan understood that he could not allow individuals to buttonhole him in other settings, or to succeed in obtaining separate action by his immediate staff. In Sacramento, to those who would nonetheless try, he would gently respond, "Well, let's round-table that."

In Washington, the much greater scale makes such a direct end-run less likely, but the problem persists in other forms. Reagan tended not to see cabinet members in one-on-one settings. The president generally dealt with them in the presence of his senior staff or other members of the cabinet. His points of discussion were often scripted in detail. Even when he did see them in less formal settings, he would tend not to engage them in separate conversations. This avoided a problem that arose, for example, under President Bush. Bush, ever the gentleman, would often socialize with cabinet members. Hearing about an issue in an informal encounter, he might communicate sympathy or support to a cabinet member, even though his immediate staff had taken a contrary approach in his name. This sometimes spawned confusion and uncertainty in the decision-making process.

Reagan insisted that the written information for decision meetings be simple, concise, and clear. As governor of California he became famous for—and was in some circles derided for—his insistence on one-page issue summaries. These "mini-memos" would include summaries of pro and con positions, along with alternative courses of action. They often included large amounts of appended materials to assist the reader, ranging from policy documents to proposed legislation, enacted statutes, newspaper articles, or whatever else might be apposite.

There are numerous benefits to this approach. As we all know from experience, it is often far easier—and reflects less sustained, disciplined thought—to write a longer rather than a shorter memorandum. The required brevity enforced a degree of preparation before presentation to a decision meeting. It ensured that the writer had placed the specific issue in the context of the overall vision and priorities of the administration. This approach also tended to arrange information in a way so that a generalist—not only Reagan as chief executive, but also other participants in the meeting—could comprehend it rapidly. At least as important, it enabled them to disentangle technical issues from broader questions of values or perspective that might otherwise have been inextricably bound up in a less disciplined presentation. Judgment and common sense could thereby make their way into the discussion, past the ramparts all too often erected by expertise.

In other cases, particularly after he became president, Reagan was offered even simpler, more graphically appealing presentations of complex issues. These ranged from cartoons concerning nuclear weapons issues to short films to a multiple-choice test on budget dilemmas. David Stockman, Reagan's first budget director, whose invincibly high self-assessment was as resilient as his characterizations of others were condescending, later wrote about a defense presentation: "It was so intellectually disreputable, so demeaning, that I could hardly bring myself to believe that a Harvard-educated cabinet officer could have brought this to the President of the United States. Did he think the White House was on Sesame Street?"

Stockman's presumptuous and overwrought reaction overlooks several factors. No chief executive of a large organization—particularly the U.S. government—can be an expert in the large variety of issues that come before him. The expertise is reposed in the staff of the organization. Simplified presentations make it possible to increase input from the chief executive and other generalists. In turn this increases the likelihood that otherwise isolated decisions can be placed in a broader context.

For Reagan, such presentations had the additional benefit of merging policy formulation with implementation. They enabled him to serve the chief executive's role as a translator of information from experts to the public, and vice versa. Reagan, with an eye toward his audience—the American people, his market—could use the meeting presentation as a template for his later public presentation. If the presentation could be made convincing to him now, he would be more likely to make a persuasive case to the public later. Reagan could begin to place the decision at hand within his broader vision, bringing to bear the unique perspective of the chief executive who must take into account actual or perceived competing priorities or questions of timing.

Viewed in this way, one can see that individuals like Stockman, for all their vaunted mastery of complexity, are themselves locked into a limited, unrealistically simplified decision process. They use numbers to create illusory certainties. Afflicted with a certain type of vanity, they do not necessarily recognize that logic and available knowledge have limitations, especially where the factors at play are changing and cannot be usefully quantified. Staffers of the Stockman mold are essential—at least until such time as they are rendered redundant by advances in personal computer software—but what they bring is rarely sufficient for making ultimate leadership decisions.

Reagan, perhaps relying more on instinct than intellect, understood this. He retained the services of Stockman and others of his ilk in the face of provocations ranging from open insubordination to self-aggrandizement intended to be at his expense. His technique of meeting management enabled the organization to obtain the value of such people without becoming hostage to their limitations.

UNAVOIDABLE MEETINGS

Every executive must take part in meetings he would prefer not to attend. There might be an urgent request from an individual or group seeking to press its case before the chief executive rather than staff. The decision may already be set in stone, and there may be many other claims on his time that are, on their face, more closely linked to achieving his priorities. Nonetheless, it may be judged important to hear out, politely, another advocate yet another time. A related situation arose in the post-election discussion between Carter and Reagan mentioned in Chapter Eight. Reagan was doubtless pleased to have the meeting, but he could not set the agenda.

This is a recurring issue for executives of large organizations with multiple constituencies. Needless to say, it arises most of all for presidents of the United States. During the recession that gripped the nation during his first term, Reagan met with New England shoe manufacturers whose industry was being destroyed by shoes pouring in from abroad. In the face of Reagan's longtime advocacy of free trade, they wanted him to change his administration's position against restricting imports. Reagan, according to one account, heard them out, but then glossed over their concerns: "Instead he launched into a lengthy reverie about how much he liked to wear cowboy boots on his ranch in Santa Barbara, finishing up with a lament about how difficult it was to find a good pair these days. The businessmen listened politely and then left, commenting among themselves that Reagan was an awfully nice man but had seemed not to follow their line of reasoning at all."

Reagan felt that he needed to accommodate the request for a meeting, but he had no intention of acceding to their demands. If the visitors' disappointment could be handled with gentleness—even at the cost of their wondering why in the world the president could not follow the unassailable logic of their argument—then that's about the best one could do. In this Reagan followed the approach Eleanor Roosevelt ascribed to his role model, her husband Franklin D. Roosevelt: "Franklin had a way, when he did not want to hear what somebody had to say, of telling stories and talking about something quite different."

A related situation arises when protocol dictates that an executive meet with a particular individual more or less on request. Viewed solely as a matter of efficiency such a meeting might usefully be delegated to staff, but as a practical matter the executive needs to honor the request. This is the situation President Reagan often faced with members of the congressional leadership.

Ed Rollins, the noted political consultant who worked in Reagan's White House and managed his 1984 reelection campaign, recounts an incident involving a senator who treated Rollins in a high-handed way. Though they were members of the same political party, the late Pennsylvania senator John Heinz was often publicly critical of the president. Nonetheless, Heinz desperately wanted Reagan's personal assistance in raising funds for his reelection campaign.

Rollins, with an unmistakable absence of enthusiasm, offered Heinz the choice of a lunch or afternoon fundraising reception. Heinz chose the reception, and lunch was scheduled for an appearance on behalf of Pennsylvania governor Richard Thornburgh. Several days later, Heinz reversed course, decided he wanted the lunch instead, and asked that Thornburgh make way for his latest preference. In the meantime, though, Thornburgh had purchased printed invitations.

Staff for the two politicians fell to bickering, and Rollins called their representatives to his office. Like a teacher dealing with quarreling children, he decided to resolve the disagreement by the flip of a coin. Thornburgh won; he elected to keep the lunch.

According to Rollins, Heinz personally called him about an hour later, "to accuse me of disrespectful behavior. 'This is no way to treat a United States senator,' he fumed, 'flipping a coin.'"

Rollins added fuel to the fire. "Senator, I just flipped another coin, and Dick Thornburgh won again. And if I flip it again, Dick Thornburgh will win again."

Heinz hung up and took his complaints over Rollins's head to Reagan's chief of staff James Baker. He demanded a meeting with the president.

Reagan's enthusiasm for this meeting must have been limited indeed. He was being asked to mediate a dispute between his staff and an important but difficult senator over a trivial matter. What is more, after being made aware of Heinz's public criticisms, Reagan called Rollins and asked, "Why are we doing *anything* for this guy?"

Rollins described the meeting:

When Heinz came in for his appeal, the president deferred to me. I made some crack about his financial situation.

"There you go," Heinz complained. "You think I'm rich. I'm not rich. I only have thirty or forty million dollars. It's my aunts and uncles who are rich." He then asserted that the president's economic policies had cost him more interest on a $300,000 personal loan he'd taken out to help pay for his last campaign.

By now Jim Baker must have wanted to go hide somewhere, and the president was astonished.

"Senator," he said, "I don't get into these things. This is Ed's call."

"Mr. President, we flipped a coin, and Dick Thornburgh got the lunch."

"Well, that sounds fair to me." An heir to the Heinz pickle fortune had overplayed his hand with a poor kid from Dixon, Illinois.

While Reagan had acceded to an essentially unavoidable meeting, he handled it so as to discourage similar demands on his time in the future. In his genial way, Reagan conveyed the message that while he would meet with the senator when necessary, such meetings would not be particularly productive from the senator's point of view. Had he done otherwise, Reagan would have encouraged Heinz and others to seek direct intervention by the president whenever they had problems with his staff's decisions. In the short run this would have increased direct demands on the president's time by raising the number of requests for such unavoidable meetings. It could also have undercut his staff's effectiveness across the board, making them afraid to act on their own. In some situations this could lead to actions not being taken that would advance the president's goals; more generally it might result in more decisions being elevated to higher levels than would truly be necessary.

All of these baleful managerial consequences could be avoided by Reagan's approach: When you are faced with an unavoidable meeting, make it substantively unproductive for the party requesting it. The executive should be courtly, listen well—but yield nothing that is not consistent with his own goals. If there is value to the requesting party in reporting to others that they simply met with the chief executive, then both sides have been well served. Otherwise, such diversions from other, better uses of the executive's time should be discouraged.

On some occasions Reagan was said to have taken a highly unconventional approach to unavoidable meetings: falling asleep. Ever since Michael Deaver publicly acknowledged in 1984 that the president sometimes nodded off in meetings, there has been a great deal of joking about Reagan's alleged daytime sleeping habits. In recent years, humorist P. J. O'Rourke has looked back with longing on the days when, in his words, sleeping with the president meant attending a cabinet meeting. In a more serious vein, it is worth noting that Reagan was never accused of being disengaged, much less nodding off, in a meeting where he considered his participation essential to achieving his priorities. Instead, by being polite but disengaged, sometimes responding only by reading note cards or telling old Hollywood stories in response to questions, Reagan convinced some congressional leaders, for example, that they could get at least as much done with his able staff without his presence. As a matter of time allocation, meeting management, and negotiating strategy, that doubtless suited Reagan just fine.

MEETINGS AS MANAGEMENT COMMUNICATION TOOLS

Meetings with chief executives necessarily do more than simply lead to a decision or pass along written information from staff. Inevitably, whenever the top person is present a meeting becomes a source of general management communications across an organization. Staff in a large enterprise, where contact is limited, tend to observe the top executive with acute curiosity. They wonder what kind of person he is, about his leadership and management style, about what his actions or appearance may signal for them and their organization. The things said and done in such meetings—including many minute details—tend to be repeated far and wide. As Peggy Noonan recalled after meeting with Reagan, "I would be able to say, 'Well I was meeting with the president the other day, and he says—' for weeks."

Small gestures become freighted with unaccustomed significance. Noonan recounted how one White House staffer was startled to hear the president quoting directly from a memorandum he had written. "The president *did* read his memos. He looked at the president, who paused and looked at [him] . . . and winked."

At another meeting, another staffer "sat along the wall in a cabinet meeting and listened as someone said something she knew to be untrue. She winced and shook her head no. She wondered if the president believed what he was hearing. She turned to look and saw him looking at her. He winked.

And the wink said, I know, I don't believe a thing this guy's saying either."

Noonan added, "We made so much of those winks." A wink or a nod or a smile or a frown can be used by a chief executive to communicate rapidly, even on issues not directly discussed. In fact, executives should remember that what they might otherwise dismiss as insignificant details are scrutinized by their team.

Other management signals are sent more directly. Noonan writes of a lunch meeting between Reagan and top members of the White House staff. In the midst of a discussion of what most of the higher-ups considered the great issues of the day, a midlevel staffer wanted the president to hear about an issue much closer to home. The valedictorian of a high school class in the South had been denied her request to speak at graduation about the importance of God in her life. Local officials apparently concluded that this would violate laws separating church and state.

After an uncomfortable silence in the room, some of the staffers slid into "tittering." On the strength of Reagan's passing glance, silence was restored. He decided on the spot to send the girl a letter of support, lauding her personal courage in the face of adversity.

Through that meeting Reagan communicated several things. He made clear that the religious concerns raised by the staffer were every bit as important as the other issues before him, and perhaps more important. He also indicated that his own respect for religious values should be reflected in the attitudes of the staff.

Attendees at meetings with the president drew inferences from everything from the colors of the jellybeans Reagan plucked from a jar to the Western décor created by the display of Remington statuettes. As we shall see in the next section, no one understood better than Reagan that effective communication requires an attention to detail in many situations other than public speeches.

REAGAN ON LEADERSHIP: MAKE MEETINGS USEFUL

- Meetings, along with the presentations and reports that accompany them, are often the greatest single time commitment of an executive. If you are to use your time—and that of your organization—well, you must use meetings well.

- An executive should decide from the beginning how he can best make his contribution, adding value through a meeting. In decision-making meetings, executives can benefit from Reagan's example. To avoid having staff adjust their presentations in an effort to please him, he would not initially reveal his own leanings.

- Encourage broad participation in decision-making meetings, including nonexperts who can inject judgment and common sense into discussions that might otherwise grant undue deference to technical expertise.

- Do not allow individuals to end-run decision-making meetings by buttonholing you in another venue.

- Keep written information simple, clear, and concise. If issues are boiled down to their essentials in one- or two-page formats, it is easier to get input from a wide variety of individuals. It can also help ensure that the matter at hand will be considered in the context of your organization's vision.

- Have staff presentations of complex issues use graphics or other user-friendly devices that allow you to begin to bridge the recommendations of technical experts with the likely questions or concerns of your ultimate consumers. An executive should be a translator between these different but mutually reliant groups.

- When meetings are unavoidable—when they are not directly relevant to achieving your goals but are nonetheless necessary for reasons such as protocol—turn them to your benefit as far as possible. To discourage additional meetings of this nature, gently make them unproductive for the other party.

- Remember that all meetings with executives become sources of management communications on issues far beyond those under consideration. Understand and direct the messages that you are sending through a wink, a gesture of support, or the emphasis you place on one matter versus another.

PART 3

COMMUNICATION

———————•••———————

[I] won a nickname, "The Great Communicator."
But I never thought it was my style or the words I used
that made a difference: It was the content. I wasn't a great
communicator, but I communicated great things.
—RONALD REAGAN, FAREWELL ADDRESS
TO THE NATION, JANUARY 11, 1989

CHAPTER 11

BECOME A SKILLED COMMUNICATOR

For years, I've heard the question: "How could an actor
be president?" I've sometimes wondered how you
could be president and not be an actor.
—RONALD REAGAN

WHEN RONALD REAGAN first sought elective
office, the governorship of California in 1966, many were
openly skeptical of his candidacy for one reason: He was an
actor. To be sure, he had had a successful career in radio, films,
and television, and as a public speaker. Nonetheless, the incumbent governor whom Reagan eventually defeated viewed
him as highly vulnerable in this regard. In a maneuver that was
memorable even by the ever-declining standards of modern
politics, Reagan's opponent commissioned a television advertisement in which he explained to a group of schoolchildren
that John Wilkes Booth, Abraham Lincoln's assassin, was also
an actor.

Communication is the place where the skills of the actor
and the leader intersect and to some extent overlap. Richard

Neustadt puts Reagan's background in perspective, observing that "Reagan was the first president to have been *professionally trained* as an actor and a televised spokesman." The majority of our most important presidents—including Washington, Lincoln, Theodore and Franklin Roosevelt, Woodrow Wilson, Dwight Eisenhower, and John Kennedy—displayed many of the talents of skilled actors in communicating with the American people.

Many business leaders also have highly developed communications skills. Longtime automotive industry executive Lee Iacocca is a powerful example. Inside the companies he served, his communication abilities doubtless helped fuel a dramatic career ascent. On the outside, he added incomparable value by his ability to communicate with the general public as well with other leaders—from Congress to Wall Street to Main Street—whose judgments would have life-or-death consequences for Chrysler Corporation in the late 1970s.

The necessity for business executives to become effective communicators is increasing by the year. Public confidence in companies and their leaders can be bolstered or shaken by the combination of 24-hour-a-day television news and the ability of millions to instantaneously obtain and interpret information from their home computers. Until recently, such information was filtered almost entirely through a small number of journalists and experts.

While few can develop the skills of Reagan, the "Great Communicator," many can certainly become recognized as skilled communicators. As we have seen throughout this book, Reagan's leadership and management skills stretched far beyond what might be dismissed as mere acting skills. At the same time, Reagan's unparalleled communication ability, reflecting years as a professional performer, made his high level of leadership and management possible.

BELIEVE IN YOUR MESSAGE

There is at least one valid reason why people might harbor reservations about entrusting a professional actor with a leadership role. An indispensable element of the actor's craft is the ability to move out of himself and convincingly assume another persona. The separation of the actor from the role he is playing unavoidably contains elements of artifice. This can cause people to wonder whether an actor ever truly leaves role-playing and expresses honest, heartfelt sentiments.

Reagan, acknowledging with some understatement that "speechmaking has played a major role in my life," added that his acting experience taught him that an actor has "to be honest in what he's doing. . . . My actor's instinct simply told me to speak the truth as I saw it and felt it." Far from convincing him that his acting training would allow him—or anyone else—to deceive others, Reagan's experience taught him the validity of the old Hollywood adage, "The camera never lies."

We all recognize when an individual is openly enthused about and committed to what he is speaking about. We also pick up unmistakable, sometimes instinctual cues when a trained advocate for hire—often a lawyer—argues forcefully on behalf of a cause in which he ultimately does not believe.

Long-time Reagan friend and informal adviser William F. Buckley Jr. is recognized as one of the most talented public speakers and debaters in America. Reflecting on the sources of Reagan's strength as a communicator, he noted Reagan's ability, after careful consideration of the merits of an issue, to convince himself of the rightness of his ultimate position. Reagan critics, of course, might see this trait from a different angle. As one observer noted of a great 19th-century British prime minister: "It is said that Mr. Gladstone could persuade most people of most things, and himself of anything." Whatever its basis, the most persuasive communicators are unquestionably, passionately committed to their cause, exuding a believability that draws others to them.

In reviewing Reagan's speeches throughout his career, this aspect comes through continually. The one great exception yet again relates to the Iran-Contra affair. He was reportedly reluctant to deliver his initial speech to the nation as the scandal unfolded in November 1986. Lou Cannon observed: "Watching the speech on television, I was struck by the validity of Reagan's long-held view about the revealing quality of the medium. All of the practiced confidence that one associates with a scripted Reagan performance was missing." This address was also poorly received by the public. Later, when Reagan acknowledged error and undertook changes in March 1987, his accompanying speech was much more assured and the public response was generally supportive.

REPETITION, REPETITION, REPETITION

If the rule for real estate is "location, location, location," the rule for a leader communicating his vision is "repetition, repetition, repetition." Reagan described one of his "theories about political speechmaking" as: "You have to keep pounding away with your message, year after year, because that's the only way it will sink into the collective consciousness. I'm a big believer in stump speeches—speeches you can give over and over and over again with slight variations. Because if you have something you believe in deeply, it's worth repeating time and again until you achieve it. You also get better at delivering it."

Reagan's rule of repetition is equally applicable to business executives and political leaders. To be sure, it may not be easy to follow, unless one has experience as a stage actor who repeats performances night after night. For most of us it is initially uncomfortable, unnatural, and monotonous.

Such negative feelings can be lessened if, following Reagan's lead, one uses repetition as an opportunity to polish the details of a presentation like those of a precious stone. From his expectation that aides would assure he had Hall's Mentholyptus available for his voice to his insistence on always having a copy of his remarks before him, Reagan left nothing to chance. Like all who perform well before an audience—from athletes to musicians to actors—it was through meticulous preparation of speeches that Reagan was able to "make it look easy."

PERSONIFY YOUR VISION

It is a truism that a significant part, if not the greatest part, of every communication is nonverbal. Much of our reaction to other people is not based on what they have said, but on our overall reaction to them. Most of us are also surprised to learn, now and again, that we have projected an impression of ourselves or our views that we would never have guessed, much less intended.

As an actor, more specifically as a film actor, Reagan had a clear sense of the images and impressions he left with others. As explained in his autobiography, *Where's the Rest of Me?*, this went back to his early experiences in Hollywood:

> The second day I was introduced to the rushes. This is the custom of going at the end of each day's work and seeing on the screen what you shot the previous day. What a shock that was! It had taken me years to get used to seeing myself as others see me; and also seeing myself instead of my mental picture of the character I'm playing. Very few of us ever see ourselves except

as we look directly at ourselves in the mirror. Thus we don't normally know how we look from behind, from the side, walking, standing, moving normally through a room. It's quite a jolt.

Reagan was keenly aware that a photograph of a public figure in an awkward moment could have a devastating effect on public confidence. Just as a well-placed anecdote can be understood as an accurate description of a large, highly complex issue, a single photographic impression of a leader can be viewed as representative of his entire character or record. The published still shot of President Carter's collapse from exhaustion after jogging became emblematic of the burn-out of his administration. The repeated images of President Ford's stumbles on stairs (despite the fact that he was probably the most talented athlete ever to hold the office) encouraged the view that his administration was hopelessly error-prone.

Reagan and his team were always conscious of the presence of a camera. His staff watched for surrounding items that might be encompassed by a camera shot. For example, in the face of opponents' charges that Reagan was a "warmonger," Michael Deaver avoided situations where a "head shot" of the president might be filmed amid military weaponry without an explanatory context. Reagan himself (as well as his wife, Nancy, a former actress in her own right) also gave careful consideration to his clothing and demeanor in important settings. Several of his former aides recall a telling incident from the 1980 presidential campaign. Following a multi-candidate Republican Party presidential debate, Reagan explained that his numerous opponents did not know how to use their hands properly when standing before an audience for an extended period. He then demonstrated his preferred approach, explaining, "What you have to do is just let your arms hang by your side, straight down. Then you curl your fingers so that they just cup your thumb."

Even in the case of debates—a setting geared more than most toward verbal exchange—Reagan emphasized the significance of nonverbal communication. Although he handled himself well against debaters ranging from Robert Kennedy to William Buckley, he performed poorly in his first televised confrontation with 1984 presidential challenger Walter Mondale. Reagan said he had been "overtrained" by his staff, who filled him to the brim with "all sorts of details, technicalities, and statistics." His view of the result is interesting: "When you're in the debate, you realize you can't command all that information and still do a good job as a debater." In addition to giving unfocused answers, his usually strong physical presence faltered. Recounting a key exchange on Medicare policy, Cannon wrote: "Reagan had been thrown on the defensive, and he looked it. As Mondale delivered his response, he looked directly at the president until Reagan dropped his eyes—something I had never seen Reagan do in any other public encounter." (Back to form in his next debate, the president recovered from this disappointing showing.)

He also made studied use of important, symbolic gestures. For example, Reagan was the first president to break traditional military protocol and routinely return salutes to military personnel in public settings. At the time he began this practice in 1981, it was interpreted as a strong message of support for a military establishment demoralized in the aftermath of the Vietnam conflict. It was also a clear reminder of the president's position as commander-in-chief of the armed forces—a never-ending challenge during the 24-hour-a-day nuclear threat of the Cold War.

Ronald Reagan was virtually always "on." One looks in vain for photographs that show him without full control over his physical presence. As president of the United States, one spends nearly every waking minute under scrutiny of cameras, staff, members of the public, and so on. The head erect and the shoulders thrown back; the purposeful stride; the familiar, lopsided smile; the jaunty wave; the empathetic listening to another's need; the respectful, confident, vigorous military salute; the hand cupping an ear as he smilingly stepped back into a waiting helicopter, freeing him from the annoyance of a pack of nettlesome reporters; the nod and the wink and the wave—these all became part of Reagan's ongoing communication with the American people. Rather than requiring conscious decision, such gestures had probably become habitual over time.

Deaver recalls an evening during Reagan's first term, when he and the president were in the office until past 11 P.M. Reagan appeared uncharacteristically exhausted in the aftermath of a contentious personnel matter—hardly his favorite use of time in any event. Saying goodnight, the president finally departed toward the living quarters, taking papers with him. As he approached the door to the Rose Garden—then of course empty and shrouded in darkness—he paused, threw his shoulders back, and resumed his unmistakable, confident stride.

In this way Reagan as leader came to personify his vision of America, embodying the presidency as he saw it (and believed others, too, wished to see it). This part of his communication armory was every bit as important as his public speaking ability. Dean Acheson, President Harry Truman's elegant and worldly secretary of state, made this connection in describing the communication genius of Winston Churchill:

> Not only was the content of his speeches wise and right but they were prepared with that infinite capacity for taking pains which is said to be genius. So was his appearance; his attitudes and gestures, his use of all the artifices to get his way, from wooing and cajolery, through powerful advocacy, to bluff bullying—all were

carefully adjusted to the need. To call this acting is quite inadequate. What we are speaking of is a transformation, a growth and a permanent change of personality.

At their highest level, well-developed communication skills of a leader are the means by which he comes to personify his vision. When a leader comes to embody a compelling vision, his tools to achieve it are multiplied exponentially, with virtually every action he takes serving as a communication to one or more sought-after audiences.

REAGAN ON LEADERSHIP: BECOME A SKILLED COMMUNICATOR

- Communication skills are essential for all who would lead organizations.

- The skills of the actor and the leader intersect—and to some extent overlap—in the area of communication.

- Always be honest in your presentations—the more deeply you believe in your message, the more believable and attractive your message becomes to others.

- When making speeches to persuade others to share your vision, remember the rule: repetition, repetition, repetition.

- Take care to ensure that the signals you send through nonverbal communications—physical movements ranging from your facial expressions to your way of walking—are consistent with and bolster your verbal message.

- Remember that nonverbal communications are properly a focus of the audience in public appearances. In considering the claims of a leader, observers often understand that the traits of character glimpsed in an "off moment" may be at least as significant as the presentation of a well-considered and rehearsed opinion on a passing matter of the day.

• If you come to embody your vision, your ability to communicate will be dramatically enhanced. When you personify your cause, virtually every action you take will send a communication to one or more audiences.

CHAPTER 12

ALWAYS FOCUS ON YOUR AUDIENCE

---◆◆◆---

The fundamental rule of public speaking, whether
on the radio, on television, or to a live crowd: Talk to
your audience, *not over their heads or through them.*
—RONALD REAGAN

ACHIEVING EXCELLENCE IN communication, like any other endeavor, requires hard work and a disciplined desire to continuously improve and learn. Almost any large bookstore in America offers numerous titles relating to public speaking, including thousands of specific suggestions. It is understandable that many people feel overwhelmed by the challenge.

In acquiring public speaking skills as a young man, Reagan recognized that rather than try to memorize hundreds of techniques, he could identify a small number of essential rules from which all the others flow. The "fundamental rule," as he saw it, is for a speaker to always talk to his audience.

At first glance, this might seem obvious. Yet it is rarely understood, much less followed with the constancy of Ronald Reagan. He understandably called it his "little secret."

Looking back, Reagan wrote that when he began broadcasting sports on WHO Radio in Des Moines, Iowa, he was quite nervous about facing a live microphone. The small, windowless studio gave him no sense of his audience. "How could I connect with all those people listening to the radio, I wondered?" He finally worked his way around the problem:

> I had a group of friends in Des Moines, and we all happened to go to the same barber. My friends would sometimes sneak away from their offices or other jobs when I was broadcasting a game and they'd get together at the barbershop and listen to it; after a while, I began to picture these friends down at the shop when I was on the air and, knowing they were there, I'd try to imagine how my words sounded to them and how they were reacting, and I'd adjust accordingly and spoke as if I was speaking personally to them. There was a specific audience out there I could see in my mind, and I sort of aimed my words at them.
>
> After I did that, something funny happened: I started getting mail from people all over the Midwest who told me I sounded as if I was talking directly and personally to *them*.

Reagan applied this lesson throughout his career: "Over the years I've always remembered that, and when I'm speaking to a crowd—or on television—I try to remember that audiences are made up of individuals, and I try to speak as if I am talking to a group of friends . . . not to millions, but to a handful of people in a living room . . . or a barbershop."

SPEAKING BEFORE LIVE AUDIENCES

Whenever possible, Reagan liked to spend time with members of his audience before delivering a speech. Michael Deaver once suggested that he could save time by skipping the dinners and lunches usually connected with such events. He could follow the lead of many other public figures, arriving just before the time his speech was scheduled to begin. Reagan declined, explaining that he preferred to use the time to get to know his audience.

For the speech itself, Reagan liked to have the first rows filled with listeners, located close enough to the podium to assure reciprocal eye contact. Kenneth Khachigian recalls an illustrative incident from Reagan's whistle-stop train tour during the 1984 reelection campaign. The train was falling behind schedule, and Khachigian worked with the president to cut the speech text. Considering proposed excisions, Reagan said that certain points must be kept, because "you should see the response I get in people's eyes when I say that." Where most speakers look at the entirety of a crowd, perhaps perceiving it as a mass, Reagan would periodically lock in and focus on one person while delivering a key line.

This required special discipline, since he was naturally very nearsighted. To facilitate his ability to glance at a written text one moment, at a specific face in a crowd in the next, Reagan applied a rather extraordinary expedient:

> I learned a trick with my contact lenses that helped me see not only my notes and the teleprompter but everything else in life. . . . I discovered that if I wore only one lens, nature sort of took over and, in effect, gave me bifocals. I wear a contact lens on my left eye but nothing over my right eye; the corrective lens over my left eye gives me 20-20 vision for seeing things over distances, while my right eye takes over at shorter range and allows me to read fine print.

In order to best inform the audience and to receive their reactions, Reagan crafted a presentation style combining the polished smoothness of studied preparation with the flexibility of spontaneity. Crossing a dais he would appear to have no written text. When he reached the lectern his left hand would deftly, almost unnoticeably remove a set of four-by-six-inch cards from a suit pocket. As he acknowledged the welcoming applause and smiled at his audience, his hands removed the rubber band holding the cards together. He would arrange the cards in the order he planned to refer to them. Throughout his speech, Reagan would glance fleetingly, almost imperceptibly at the cards. Each contained a series of key points that Reagan had written in a sort of homemade shorthand. The cards could easily be rearranged, edited, or updated before or even during a speech if necessary, to reflect information or questions Reagan might pick up from an audience. He viewed his approach as a compromise between reading a speech aloud—which does not "hold an audience"—and trying "to memorize every word you wanted to say" (which also takes the speaker's attention from his audience).

Reagan would also directly learn the concerns of his live audiences through question-and-answer sessions following his speeches. This reflected his awareness that most audiences do not like to sit passively as a speaker continues interminably—he believed twenty minutes to be the maximum people should be expected to sit in "respectful silence." As with other aspects of his public speaking, this became his *modus operandi* during his years as spokesman for the General Electric Company, touring plants across America in the 1950s.

In part as a response to attacks from political opponents who tried to turn his skilled speechmaking against him—saying he was merely an actor reading someone else's lines—gubernatorial candidate Reagan used question-and-answer sessions to break the emerging tradition of the methodically cocooned, consultant-driven candidate. He later wrote: "Whether the campaign audience was three or three thousand, I'd make a few remarks, then take questions. I hadn't planned it that way, but this turned out to be a wonderful way to learn about the issues that were on people's minds." As a result, for example, Reagan was ahead of pollsters and pundits in sensing the inchoate public demand for restoration of order on college campuses then roiled by student demonstrations.

Reagan found that some of the most important audience suggestions and reactions came from individuals who waited to talk with him after his speeches. Veteran Reagan aide Peter Hannaford recalls accompanying him to a Lincoln Day dinner address in the mid-1970s. Members of the audience streamed to the head table after dinner, seeking to have their programs autographed or to get in a thought or a question. Seeing that it was getting quite late—concerned because they had to leave early the next morning—Hannaford tried without success to pull Reagan away. Reagan gently disagreed, saying, "We'll just stay and do this until we're finished."

He would also give his full attention to individuals—including children—whom he met during his travels. Whoever was in his audience, whether one or one hundred, would receive his complete, undivided attention. And he would try to leave them satisfied.

MASTER EVERY AVAILABLE MEDIUM

Applying Reagan's rule to live audience presentations can improve many people's speaking ability rapidly, simply by moving them from a disabling *self-consciousness* to an empowering *audience-consciousness*. But the rule has other implications, as well.

Many people master one medium of communication: the written word, the still photograph, television, radio, short videos, speeches before large audiences, or presentations to small groups. Very few master all of them; even fewer can perform flexibly in changing settings. Those few who can, such as Ronald Reagan, add immeasurably to the power of their message.

The key, in each case, is focusing on the audience. Reagan early on had a vivid sense of the possibilities of radio, which he called "theater of the mind." He started out working as a sports announcer, and much later he became a commentator on current events in the years between his governorship and his presidency. During his presidency he began a tradition of Saturday morning radio addresses, inspired by the "fireside chats" of his idol, Franklin Roosevelt.

In the case of television, as with motion pictures and other visual media, Reagan had a strong sense of his own appearance on the screen and was well attuned to audience reaction. He also had confidence in his ability to communicate through the written word, either in articles or in personal replies to letters from members of the public, which he wrote from his days as a young actor through his terms as president.

When one habitually focuses on the audience, the resulting changes in emphasis make it possible to communicate simply and successfully.

MULTIPLE AUDIENCES

Increasingly, executives—like political leaders—face multiple audiences. This occurs, for example, when a speech before a live audience is also televised or taped for radio. Where the speaker's style is, like Reagan's, rather intimate (unlike that of the traditional barnburner political speaker), it may lend itself, with minimal adjustment, to the needs of both media.

A question that may arise in a performance before any large audience, or where more than one medium is involved, is *which* audience one should address. Anyone at a high level of public or private sector accountability must discern and evaluate this choice with care. This is a critical matter that Reagan handled with consummate skill.

In 1976, looking back on the 1966 election campaign that ended his own career in public life, former California governor Pat Brown made a trenchant observation:

> Reagan leaves little doubt that he is constantly aware of the big audience. Most politicians tend to relate—logically and emotionally—to the individual reporter who is asking questions, or a bit more broadly with the newspaper he represents. Reagan relates primarily and continuously with the television audience. As a trained actor, he is able to ignore the clutter of equipment and commotion of reporters at a press conference and keep his eye and a good part of his mind on the audience represented by the small lens of the camera.

Virtually every public speaking opportunity presents a choice, whether recognized or not, among several audiences. The primary audience to which one should communicate might be based on any number of factors—how many people are included, their influence as opinion leaders, and so on. Generally, in the case of a major public communication, the speaker will choose to aim his attention to the broad audience made possible by television, as opposed to focusing solely on a much smaller live audience.

In some situations, particularly in an important speech, the speaker may aim parts of his message at different audiences. This was illustrated vividly in Reagan's 1980 acceptance speech at the Republican National Convention. Most of the address was aimed at unifying various factions within his own political party in preparation for the autumn campaign. At the end, however, Reagan changed direction:

> The time is now to redeem promises once made to the American people by another candidate, in another time and another place. He said:

"For three long years I have been going up and down this country preaching that government—Federal, state and local— costs too much. I shall not stop that preaching. As an immediate program of action, we must abolish useless offices. We must eliminate unnecessary functions of government.

"We must consolidate subdivisions of government and, like the private citizen, give up luxuries which we can no longer afford." And then he said:

"I propose to you my friends, and through you, that government of all kinds, big and little, be made solvent and that the example be set by the President of the United States and his Cabinet."

Those were Franklin Delano Roosevelt's words as he accepted the Democratic nomination for President in 1932.

The time is now, my fellow Americans, to recapture our destiny, to take it into our own hands.

By praising Roosevelt by name, as well as using his language both in quotations and on his own—"to recapture our destiny" evoked the "rendezvous with destiny" of FDR's 1936 renomination acceptance speech—Reagan was reaching out from the convention hall to millions of Americans watching at home on television. Many of them would later become known as "Reagan Democrats."

In closing, he offered his hand toward another group watching from afar, evangelical Christians and other Americans troubled by the increasing separation of religion from public life:

I'll confess that I've been a little afraid to suggest what I'm going to suggest. I'm more afraid not to. Can we begin our crusade joined together in a moment of silent prayer?

God bless America.

Thank you.

YOUR AUDIENCE IS YOUR CUSTOMER

To become an effective public speaker, you should consider members of your audience to be your customers. You must strive to make certain, as Reagan did, that they leave satisfied they received value for their time and money. If you focus on matters unrelated to your audience—your personal thoughts or appearance, your company or industry, your competition, or anything else—you are not likely to achieve recognition as a skilled communicator. On the other hand, if you methodically focus on your audience, tapping into the power of Reagan's "secret," you will find that many of the complexities of public speaking are dramatically simplified.

REAGAN ON LEADERSHIP: ALWAYS FOCUS ON YOUR AUDIENCE

- Remember Reagan's "fundamental rule of public speaking": Always talk to your audience.

- When communicating through any medium—print, television, radio—aim your message as you would to a group of familiar individuals in a familiar setting.

- When you focus methodically on the interests and concerns of your audience, many questions about presentation—how long to speak, what to emphasize, and so on—take care of themselves.

- When you appear before a live audience, make use of all available opportunities before and after your speech—including question-and-answer periods—to learn more about your audience's perspectives.

- Develop a speaking style that allows you to combine the benefits of careful preparation with the flexibility of spontaneity, so that you can perceive and react to the audience's response during your presentation.

- Give your complete attention to any audience, whether one hundred eminent personages or one small child.

- Recognize that when you face multiple audiences, as when there is television coverage of a live speech, you have a choice of which audience to emphasize.

- If you are speaking to a large audience, you can consciously choose to speak to several parts of your audience at various points in your presentation.

- If you wish to excel as a public speaker, think of your audience as your customers. Speak, to the greatest possible extent, in a manner and on a topic that interests your audience.

CHAPTER 13

BECOME YOUR OWN BEST SPEECHWRITER

Reagan was his own best speechwriter.
—MARTIN ANDERSON

MANY HAVE OBSERVED that we are living in a time
of unprecedented opportunities for communication, yet the
quality of public speaking is in marked decline. Business
executives and political leaders speak more than ever, but they
seem to say less and less. One senses that many do not even
write the words they read aloud to the rest of us.

Outstanding public speakers share one practice: They
write their own speeches. The qualities that make a speaker
effective—particularly his belief in what he is saying, and his
relentless focus on audience—are greatly enhanced when the
speaker is also his own speechwriter. It is not coincidental that
leaders who personify their visions have often prepared their
speeches with great care. The discipline placed on thoughts
by the process of writing, combined with the mixing of the
author's personality into the choice of words and cadences,
adds clarity and holds the prospect of originality.

Perhaps because of his background as a professional
actor, as well as the high public profile assumed by some of his

White House speechwriters, many people do not realize the extent to which Reagan wrote his own speeches. In the years prior to his presidency, he drafted most of his speeches—and when he did receive assistance, he did not hesitate to revise or rewrite until he was satisfied with the result.

In the White House the demands on a president's time are staggering, and there are a large number of occasions requiring some presidential comment. Speechwriters are a necessity. Nonetheless, Reagan remained very much involved in writing major addresses, which as we have seen he used as policy-making tools. His many years as a professional communicator—including his radio commentaries, articles, and speeches—constituted an immense resource from which his staff could draw both the president's substance and style. As Peggy Noonan recalled, "The president's stand on any given issue was usually a matter of record. He'd been in politics twenty years, and his basic philosophy wasn't exactly a secret." When one reads the speeches of Reagan over the years—from public and private life, assisted by various staff—one cannot help but notice that he was saying much the same thing, in much the same way, over and over and over again.

SPEECH STRUCTURE AND CHOICE OF WORDS

Reagan employed a traditional speech structure: "Here's my formula: I usually start with a joke or a story to catch the audience's attention; then I tell them what I am going to tell them, I tell them, and then I tell them what I told them."

He followed several personal rules for writing effective speeches. One was his preference for short sentences. He also favored short words: "Don't use a word with two syllables if a one-syllable word will do." The key—as always—was to communicate his vision in a way that would be understood by his audience: "Use simple language. . . . Remember, there are people out there sitting and listening, they've got to be able to absorb what I'm saying."

Many of Reagan's memorable phrases exemplify his adherence to this rule. Student protesters should "obey the rules or get out." "In the present crisis, government is not the solution to our problem; government is the problem." The Soviet Union was an "Evil Empire." "Mr. Gorbachev, tear down this wall!" Equivocation invariably slides speakers toward circumlocution and a profusion of conditioning words and phrases. Reagan's words were invariably short, often judgmental, and familiar in everyday usage.

USE EXAMPLES TO BUTTRESS YOUR CASE

Another important Reagan rule for speechwriters: "If you can, use an example. An example is better than a sermon." Among the types of examples he employed to great effect: statistics, quotations from historical and current events, graphic representations, and anecdotes of individual accomplishments.

The speech that unmistakably illuminated Reagan's potential as a political leader—his October 27, 1964, televised address supporting Barry Goldwater's doomed presidential candidacy—employed many illustrative statistics. Reagan used numerical examples to illustrate the tax collector's share of an individual worker's wages ("37 cents out of every dollar"); the folly of proposed juvenile delinquency centers said to cost $4,700 per year ("We can send them to Harvard for $2,700!"); and the unnecessary waste of federal welfare policy ("We are spending $45 billion on welfare. Now do a little arithmetic, and you will find that if we divided the $45 billion equally among those 9 million poor families, we would be able to give each family $4,600 a year, and this added to their present income should eliminate poverty!").

In 1981, Reagan's first major speech from the Oval Office made the case for a new economic policy with numerous examples intended to make complex issues plain by rendering them in the shared language and experience of everyday life. The fact that there were seven million Americans out of work meant that "if they stood in a line, allowing three feet for each person, the line would reach from Maine to California." Holding a dollar bill and some coins, he explained the costs of inflation: "Here is a dollar such as you earned, spent, or saved in 1960. And here is a quarter, a dime, and a penny—thirty-six cents. That's what this 1960 dollar is worth today. And if the present world inflation rate should continue three more years, that dollar of 1960 will be worth a quarter."

In a similar vein, former senator Eugene McCarthy remembered sharing a podium with Reagan in 1975. "I recall him saying that if the dollar bills representing the total [national] debt were stitched end-to-end they would reach the moon and back two or three times. The audience seemed quite taken by his examples."

Perhaps the most stirring examples were those relating to personal heroism. In his first inaugural address, after paying homage to Washington and other "monumental men" who were memorialized on the Capital Mall, Reagan characteristically turned to the thousands of Americans who had made the ultimate sacrifice in wartime.

> Under one such marker lies a young man, Martin Treptow, who left his job in a small town barbershop in 1917 to go to France with the famed Rainbow Division. There, on the western front, he was killed trying to carry a message between battalions under heavy artillery fire.
>
> We're told that on his body was found a diary. On the fly-leaf under the heading "My Pledge," he had written these words:

"America must win this war. Therefore I will work, I will save, I will sacrifice, I will endure, I will fight cheerfully and do my utmost, as if the issue of the whole struggle depended on me alone."

In a ritual adopted by his successors, Reagan used the occasion of his annual state of the union address to present individual Americans whose courage or other achievements illustrated the best in the American character. In 1982, he praised Lenny Skutnik, who had risked his own life by diving into icy waters to save the life of another following an airplane crash near Washington, D.C. Skutnik, seated in a place of honor with Reagan's immediate family, was showcased as an American hero. After the invasion of Grenada, the president paid a similar tribute to the heroism of Sergeant Stephen Trujillo. In addition to inspiring his countrymen, Trujillo would personify Reagan's conviction that the Caribbean military intervention in which he participated was consistent with American values.

USE STORIES TO MAKE YOUR POINT

The Treptow, Skutnik, and Trujillo examples of heroism were each part of larger stories Reagan built around the incidents for which they were honored. Reagan understood that stories could be exceptionally effective in communicating important issues. They could present controversial or delicate matters without necessarily personalizing them. Merely by using phrases other than those customarily heard in discussion, a speaker can communicate important points to the listener that might otherwise be ignored, missed, or dismissed when couched in words heavily laden with history or negative associations.

When Reagan spoke to students at Moscow State University in 1988, he used stories as a means to overcome distances created by language differences, age, culture, history and experience. Making the case for the inevitable triumph of the economic freedom then beginning to sweep the world, he explained:

> The fact is, bureaucracies are a problem around the world. There's an old story about a town—it could be anywhere—with a bureaucrat who is known to be a good-for-nothing, but somehow had always hung on to power. So one day, in a town meeting, an old woman got up and said to him: "There is a folk legend here where I come from that when a baby is born, an angel comes down from heaven and kisses it on one part of its body. If the angel kisses him on his hand, he becomes a handyman. If he kisses him on his forehead, he becomes bright and clever. And I've been trying to figure out where the angel kissed you so that you should sit there for so long and do nothing."

The audience laughed—but they listened, too. When a story manages to convey an element of truth in a universal, humorous form, it gathers additional power by the likelihood that it will be told and retold by others into the future. Perhaps in part for the same reason, Reagan, like many other storytellers, occasionally exercised some license with the supporting facts—not to mislead on the main point, but to better illustrate it. For example, the Treptow story was presented by Reagan in the context of a reference to Arlington National Cemetery, though Treptow was actually buried in Wisconsin. While not technically inaccurate, the line from his inaugural address could be viewed as misleading. Reagan is reported to have personally made the decision to present the story in this way because it was "theatrically imposing."

ALWAYS HOLD THE PEN

A key tenet in any negotiation where language is at issue is that a party should seek to always hold the pen. Others will have input, but in the end preponderant power flows to the one who writes the words.

In a similar way, Reagan always held the pen in preparing his speeches. Consistent with his passive management style, as president he would not necessarily comment or react if a draft suited his needs. On the other hand, if he were dissatisfied he would not hesitate to express his wishes or rewrite something himself if necessary. Whether a speechwriter was preparing a text based on Reagan's voluminous prior public utterances—or if the president himself prepared or edited a presentation—Reagan always held the pen for his speeches. That fact, as much as anything else, was a source of his great power to communicate.

Anyone seeking to become a skilled communicator should consider Reagan's example. Where a speech faithfully reflects the speaker's strongly held vision—and is expressed in the speaker's own words—it can be infused with compelling spirit and energy. Whether you are an executive with access to speechwriting assistance or an individual looking for inspiration in the outstanding speeches of others, it is important to aim to be your own best speechwriter. If you take it seriously, it is a goal for which you are assured success.

REAGAN ON LEADERSHIP: BE YOUR OWN BEST SPEECHWRITER

- To become a skilled public speaker, find your own voice and become your own best speechwriter.

- When speaking to a large audience, use short sentences and short words. Your listeners are most likely to absorb simple language.

- Whenever possible, use examples—statistics, quotations, stories, and graphics—to make your points. Examples drawn from everyday experience can often explain complex issues more readily than abstract argument, however logical. If your examples are sufficiently interesting, they can gain additional power when listeners repeat your examples to others.

- Even if you have the assistance of others in gathering ideas for writing a speech (including studying others' successful work), be sure that you "hold the pen" for the final product.

CHAPTER 14

RESPONDING TO CRITICS AND CRITICISM

I never pay much attention to critics.
—RONALD REAGAN, 1987

Speak the affirmative; emphasize your choice
by utter ignoring of all that you reject.
—RALPH WALDO EMERSON

ALL LEADERS—from scout troops to large corporations—must be prepared for questioning and criticism. Some criticisms will be accurate and can enable continual improvement. Others might be off base but nonetheless add value at least in letting you know that your communications must improve. And some may be malicious, intentionally misleading, or altogether false. The ability to deal with critics and criticism in all their manifestations is a key to effective leadership.

As in other areas, Reagan credited his movie experience with providing him some perspective:

When you've been in the profession I was in, you get accustomed to criticism in the press—true and untrue, fair and unfair—and learn to take what you read about yourself and others with a big dose of salt. Gossip columnists and critics become a part of your life. A picture you've made may be panned by a critic and you'll say to yourself, "You know, that's a pretty good movie and the audience likes it." It teaches you that the press isn't always right, and prepares you for criticism in politics; you develop a skepticism about what you read, and you take it in stride.

An unconventional leader who made his way to the top level of politics in his first run for elective office—advancing an agenda that threatened the institutions and individuals benefiting from the status quo—Reagan inevitably occasioned controversy. He generally handled it with aplomb. Frustrated opponents gave him nicknames such as the "Great Deflector" and, most famously, the "Teflon President."

CONFRONT CRITICISM DIRECTLY

Reagan encountered hostile territory as he made his way from Hollywood to Sacramento. While he doubtless benefited from being a known face—and from being underestimated by some adversaries—he also confronted skepticism, condescension, and withering criticism. Incumbant-governor Pat Brown, perhaps finding it difficult to credibly offer positive change after eight years in office, openly ridiculed the notion of an actor seated at the head of councils of power.

Reagan proved a tough quarry. With roundhouse, lunging attacks, Brown was trying to lure the novice into the political equivalent of *Championship Wrestling*. Instead, Reagan took the vantage point of the audience both were attempting to reach. Reagan chose to present himself as what he was: "an ordinary citizen who wanted to start unraveling the mess politicians were making of our government." With an unusual combination of high self-confidence and lack of vanity, he responded to Brown: "Sure, the man who has the job has more experience than anyone else . . . that's why I'm running."

When Senator Edward Kennedy of Massachusetts traveled to California to assist Brown, he expressed dismay that "Reagan has never held any political office before and here he is seeking the top spot in the government of California." Reagan dispatched him almost effortlessly: "I understand there's a senator from Massachusetts who's come to California and he's concerned that I've never held office prior to seeking this job. Well, you know, come to think of it, the senator from Massachusetts never held *any* job before he became a senator."

At the same time, Reagan recognized that there were legitimate concerns about both his lack of experience in politics and his acting background. As we have seen, his reliance on question-and-answer periods with audiences was in part to assuage such doubts. To prepare for such sessions, as well as other unscripted encounters, Reagan undertook what amounted to a crash course on the major issues facing the state, as well as policy options. Later, seeking the presidency in 1980, he again turned to question-and-answer periods as a way to lessen perceived skittishness among Easterners considering the prospect of a Californian in the White House. He took a similar approach to questions about his age, responding by compressing his campaign calendar, working conspicuously long hours, and so on.

USE HUMOR TO RESPOND TO CRITICISM

One of Reagan's most effective techniques for dealing with criticism was his use of humor. By making himself the butt of jokes he would subtly affect the discussion of the underlying issue. He also separated himself from the many would-be leaders who take themselves too seriously. His use of humor also reflected his continual concentration on his audience, rather than on his opponent.

Perhaps the most famous use of such humor in American political history occurred in Reagan's second 1984 debate against opponent Walter Mondale. Following a halting, occasionally disoriented performance in their first debate, Reagan, aged 73, had to confront directly what some called the "senility factor." One of the reporters' questions indeed raised the issue, none too lightly. Rather than view it as an affront, Reagan understood that it reflected legitimate and widespread public concern and could therefore be viewed as a welcome opportunity.

Looking earnestly at the reporter, with a hint of a smile, he provided a comprehensive response to the concerns of millions of Americans with just a few well-chosen words: "I want you to know that also I will not make age an issue of this campaign. I am not going to exploit for political purposes my opponent's youth and inexperience."

His answer led to an explosion of laughter in the studio audience—inevitably eliciting an apparently affectionate chuckle from Mondale himself—and reassured millions of Americans. Being part of Reagan's audience ourselves, perhaps we can be forgiven some skepticism of his subsequent recollection, "My answer to the question just popped off the top of my head. I'd never anticipated it, nor had I thought in advance what my answer might be to such a question."

Reagan also used humor in handling other widespread questioning and criticism. Against the backdrop of Washington workaholism (and previously in Sacramento), he dismissed caviling about his conspicuously regular hours: "They say that hard work never killed anyone, but I figure, why take the chance?" Though some pointed to his modest educational attainments as a weakness, he was unabashed: "I let football and other extracurricular activities eat into my study time with the result that my grade average was closer to the C level required for eligibility than it was to straight A's. And even now [as president of the United States] I wonder what I might have accomplished if I'd studied harder."

DO NOT PERSONALIZE CRITICISM

Sometimes it is hard not to take public criticism personally —and it may also be difficult to resist the temptation to personally criticize someone else. Nonetheless, as Reagan's experience shows, it is best not to personalize criticism in either direction.

In March 1966, when Reagan was in the early stages of his campaign for the Republican nomination for governor, he lost his temper and walked out of a public meeting at which his two opponents repeatedly labeled him a racist. Lyn Nofziger recalled the scene: "'Sons of bitches,' he muttered angrily, but loudly enough to be heard in the audience. Then he crumpled a piece of paper he was holding, flipped it into the audience, and stalked off the stage, muttering oaths under his breath." Although Reagan eventually returned to a cocktail party at the end of the day, a subsequent press account made mention only of his apparently petulant behavior. To make things worse, long-time *Los Angeles Times* cartoonist Paul Conrad immortalized the incident. Referring to Reagan's most famous movie as well as his newly published campaign autobiography, *Where's the Rest of Me?*, he depicted the aspiring politician holding his head under his arm, asking, "Where's the rest of me?"

The fallout from this incident was so severe that at least one of Reagan's most important backers had to be persuaded not to abandon the nascent candidacy he had helped create. In addition to learning that it was not acceptable to "explode in response to [an] attack on my personal integrity," Reagan became quite sophisticated in responding to criticism.

Throughout 1966, as the candidate burdened with the fewest conventional qualifications for high office—but with evident and undeniable promise as a campaigner—he inevitably became the target of attacks from competing politicians. With the tacit support of the officially neutral state Republican Party chairman, Reagan gratefully adopted what the chairman called the "Eleventh Commandment: Thou shalt not speak ill of any fellow Republican." This approach, which Reagan expressed throughout the remainder of his career, served his immediate interests and over time elevated him above the usual pack of negative campaigners.

He recognized that premeditated and exceptionally harsh attacks, such as Brown's infamous television advertisement associating Reagan with the actor who assassinated Lincoln, reflected desperation rather than strength. If he avoided responding in kind, the attack might be viewed by the audience as more illuminating about the critic than the intended target. Haynes Johnson reports that as the 1966 campaign entered its final days, Reagan was in San Francisco preparing to speak to the Commonwealth Club when Nofziger was told about the Brown commercial.

Smelling blood, the reporters pressed Nofziger for immediate reaction from Reagan. He hadn't heard about it, Nofziger told them.

"So I went and found him at the head table," Nofziger recalled. "I went up and got him aside, and I said, 'Brown has apparently said something to the effect that it was an actor who shot Lincoln. I think you ought to play it very cool. Don't get mad or be shocked about it.'"

"Don't worry, don't worry," he says Reagan replied.

Reagan delivered his speech without mentioning the Brown statement. Immediately after, the reporters pressed forward. Had he heard that Governor Brown had just said that it was an actor who shot Lincoln? they shouted. What did he think about that?

Reagan looked startled. "Pat said that?" he finally said. "Why, I can't believe that. Pat wouldn't say anything like that. I wouldn't want to comment on that until I hear further."

Kirk West, who served in the Reagan administration in Sacramento, recounts how Governor Reagan dealt with two persistent critics in the state capitol:

> I recall that, at one point, Jesse Unruh and George Moscone, the respective State Assembly and Senate leaders—both Democrats—were carrying on in a concerted and coordinated attack on Reagan. I don't recall the particular issue, only that they appeared to be very angry.
>
> The press secretary and our people from the Department of Finance furnished the information to rebut what Unruh and Moscone were claiming, along the lines of, "They say this has increased by 14 percent when it's only gone up by 8 percent"— that sort of thing. We had all the statistical refutations and Reagan absorbed them all.
>
> Reagan went across the hall to the press conference room and the first question was, "What do you think of the charges of Senator Moscone and Assembly Speaker Unruh?" And, Reagan says, "Well, I thought George was at his best when he was terribly angry and Jesse was at his best when he was terribly hurt." The reporters roared with laughter.

Where you believe that charges are without merit, it is sometimes useful to follow Reagan's example in not granting them any unjustified credibility. This is especially apt in situations where reporters might simply print the opposing views as if they deserved equal consideration. Far from reacting personally or responding in kind, he pulled away, using gentle humor to throw light on the overall situation.

In 1980, running for the presidency, he again faced an incumbent who chose to run a negative campaign that was highly critical of Reagan personally. Rather than respond in kind, Reagan remained on a higher plane, culminating in a televised debate with his immortal response to a Carter fusillade alleging lack of commitment to Medicare: "There you go again."

As a former actor, Reagan recognized that personal attacks are often aimed at leaders in their symbolic roles or as representatives of institutions, rather than as individuals. Such attacks are not "personal" in the usual sense. Likewise, the responses should not be from the leader's personal standpoint, either; he should be cognizant that he is representing a vision, an idea, or an institution.

As Reagan later wrote, he and his adversary Tip O'Neill developed an approach designed to protect their personal relationship from their representative roles:

> I called him and said, "Tip, I just read in the paper what you said about me yesterday. I though we had a pretty fine relationship going . . ."
>
> "Ol' buddy," Tip said, "that's politics. After six o'clock we can be friends; but before six, it's politics."
>
> . . . So, after a while, whenever I'd run into him, whatever time it was, I'd say, "Look Tip, I'm resetting my watch; it's six o'clock."

EMPHASIZE THE AFFIRMATIVE

As Douglas Bailey, noted political consultant and creator of the presidential *Hotline*, recalls, Reagan as leader "often played to bad reviews." Clark Clifford, erstwhile *éminence grise* of official Washington, marked the Californian's arrival with the oft-quoted epithet "amiable dunce." Some who shared Reagan's general political approach were vitriolic when he strayed from orthodoxy. As he achieved nuclear arms reduction, one self-styled conservative slandered him with a well-known Russian Communist term: "useful idiot." Pete Wilson —who worked with him successively as an assemblyman, mayor, and U.S. Senator, and ultimately following him as California's governor—observed that one source of Reagan's power was that he "was able to take a punch."

Reagan rarely displayed public anger in response to such provocations (unless they included his family, which he considered out of bounds). Instead, he remained invincibly genial. He focused intently on his vision and on the audience he was trying to reach. He understood that replying in kind to the personal attacks could only distract and detract from that effort. Having become the personification of his vision, Reagan also knew that many people would make judgments about what he *said* based on their confidence in what he *was*.

Criticism did not throw Reagan off course. He did not allow it to. He would respond to it, if at all, in the context of his own message. He could brush off even the most personal of attacks because his pursuit of leadership was in the service of his vision. With a successful Hollywood career behind him—and having withstood the inevitable ups and downs— Reagan in no sense needed public office to ratify his own worth in anyone's eyes.

Reagan's singular ability to handle critics and criticism provides a window on the unique mix of personal traits that characterize his overall approach to leadership—authenticity, faith, courage, humility, perseverance, discipline, grace, and distance. In the next section, we will consider such traits.

REAGAN ON LEADERSHIP: RESPONDING TO CRITICS AND CRITICISM

- Anyone who aspires to leadership must not only accept questioning and criticism but also learn from it.

- As you ascend to higher levels of leadership, and as you raise the stakes of your endeavor, questioning and criticism should—and will—become more intense.

- Respond directly to legitimate criticism, but use great care before responding to the critic. Do not allow personal attacks to distract you from focusing on your audience rather than on your adversaries.

- When you respond to hostile criticism, respond in terms consistent with your broader message rather than in the terms of the critic.

- React in a studied, detached manner—rather than with uncontrolled anger—in response to inaccurate or unfair attacks. Do not inadvertently add your own credibility to the attack.

- Emphasize the affirmative rather than the negative wherever possible. Focus on what you are *for*—and ignore what you are *against*.

PART 4

SELF-MANAGEMENT

---•••---

It is not difficult to understand how it comes
about that, in different periods, character should
sometimes be sought and sometimes kept at arm's length.
When times are good and men can take life easily,
they will pay lip service to that uncomfortable virtue,
but will have no recourse to it. But all the world
will clamor for it when danger threatens.
—CHARLES DE GAULLE, *THE EDGE OF THE SWORD*

One man cannot do right in one department
of life whilst he is occupied in doing wrong in any
other department. Life is one indivisible whole.
—MAHATMA GANDHI

CHAPTER 15

REAGAN'S PERSONAL TRAITS: LEADERSHIP AS A WAY OF LIFE

If no one among us is capable of governing himself,
then who among us has the capacity to govern someone else?
—RONALD REAGAN, FIRST INAUGURAL ADDRESS
AS GOVERNOR OF CALIFORNIA, 1967

W E LIVE IN a time of great skepticism—even cynicism—about leaders and leadership. Some prominent leaders in government and business appear to be little more than sophisticated wirepullers, making organizations work for the benefit of themselves and those around them but heedless of obligations to the broader community. One consequence: Even when apparently positive action is taken, many journalists and armchair critics spend more time speculating about self-interested motivations than considering the substantive matters in question.

In considering a spectacular career such as Reagan's, one is tempted to search for "the story behind the story." What one finds, however, is at once more mundane and more significant. A number of those who knew him best described him with the same line: "With Ronald Reagan what you see is what you get." Perhaps against our initial presuppositions concerning a leader who had been a professional actor, his personality was marked by an unquestionable *integrity*—a word derived from the Latin for "whole" or "complete." As Stephen Covey explains: "Integrity includes but goes beyond honesty. Honesty is telling the truth—in other words, *conforming our words to reality*. Integrity is *conforming reality to our words*—in other words, keeping promises and fulfilling expectations. This requires an integrated character, a oneness, primarily with self but also with life."

As with all leaders of consequence, Reagan's ability to lead others was an outgrowth of his ability to govern himself; as with all people, his own life was not flawless. Nonetheless, Reagan's personal traits were exemplary in ways that have application in times and places beyond his own.

COURAGE

As Winston Churchill wrote, "Courage is rightly esteemed the first of human qualities because it is the quality which guarantees all the others." Reagan demonstrated various forms of courage through the course of his life.

Beginning as a young lifeguard, he exhibited physical courage. In the 1940s he ignored threats of violence and facial disfigurement from opponents of his anti-Communist leadership in Hollywood. During the turbulence of the 1960s, when protests were often interspersed with violence, he confronted demonstrators and made a point of not adjusting his plans in response to threats.

Napoleon Bonaparte wrote of another dimension: "As to moral courage, I have very rarely met with the two o'clock in the morning kind. I mean unprepared courage, that which is necessary on the unexpected occasion, and which, in spite of the most unforeseen events, leaves full freedom of judgment and decision." With more aptness than anyone could have imagined, Prime Minister Margaret Thatcher of Great Britain, on the occasion of her first visit to Reagan as president in February 1981, wished him "two o'clock in the morning courage" during her official toast.

Just over a month later, on March 30, 1981, the new president, age 70, was shot in the lung during an assassination attempt. Arriving at a Washington, D.C., hospital, Reagan managed to walk into the emergency room before collapsing. While the nation looked on in dread, facing the possible loss of yet another public figure to violence, Reagan provided reassurance through a succession of apparently insouciant one-liners. Moving in and out of consciousness, he felt a nurse's hand gripping his own, and asked: "Does Nancy know about us?"

When he finally saw Nancy, he used heavyweight boxer Jack Dempsey's line to his own wife following his defeat by Gene Tunney: "Honey, I forgot to duck." As a doctor prepared to operate, Reagan cracked, "I hope you're a Republican." When he emerged from the recovery room early the next morning, a tube in his throat made speaking difficult. Instead, the president sent a series of handwritten notes to concerned aides. "I'd like to do this scene again—starting at the hotel." "Winston Churchill said there is no more exhilarating feeling than being shot at without result." "Send me to L.A. where I can see the air I'm breathing."

This show of courage in the most grievous circumstances endeared Reagan to the American people. His embodiment of his vision became uniquely complete and compelling. And his movie persona of the courageous, very American "Gipper" fused into his role as president. This association was enhanced when Reagan spoke at Notre Dame, along with Pat O'Brien (another actor from *Knute Rockne: All American*), shortly after the assassination attempt.

Courage—physical, moral, political—marks the entirety of Reagan's career. From his willingness to stand virtually alone against conventional opinion to his decision to challenge an incumbent president of the United States for his party's nomination to his successful negotiations for nuclear arms reduction with the Soviet Union, he demonstrated this indispensable character trait.

AUTHENTICITY

When one takes into account the development of strong traits of character, it becomes clear that every leader, regardless of economic background, is in a sense self-made. At the same time, those who are most effective are also the most authentic. This makes others comfortable investing a high degree of trust in the leader; it is the source of believability. In the words of Samuel Taylor Coleridge, "What comes from the heart, goes to the heart."

It was by no means unreasonable for people to initially question the authenticity of a prospective leader who had been a professional actor. In retrospect, one of Reagan's most significant actions in this regard may have been his "spot decision" as a young, aspiring film actor to keep his own name rather than allow a Hollywood press agent to make up a new one.

Reagan became known for portraying one character type in the movies: the wholesome, handsome, heroic, guileless, steady American "good guy." This role was consistent with his real-life personality. His one film venture against type did not work out well. Reagan later explained, "A lot of people who went to see *The Killers*, I'm told, kept waiting for me to turn out to be a good guy in the end and dispatch the villains in the last reel, because that's how they had always seen me before. But I didn't, and for whatever reason, the picture didn't ring any bells."

Reagan deployed the artifices of the actor to better convey his authenticity. This is not so surprising when one considers that such artifices are merely a means to communicate a credible picture to a larger audience than could be reached otherwise. As Peggy Noonan explained, "He was really acting but the part he played was Ronald Reagan."

CONFIDENCE AND OPTIMISM

Reagan was notable for his optimism—it was a keystone of his political philosophy, his personality, and his approach to leadership. Some saw his insistent focus on the bright side of things as what might be called overweening optimism; they viewed it as misleading if not dangerous in gliding over the negative, the uncertain, or the disagreeable. For example, his political philosophy assumed that individual Americans doing the right things in their daily lives on issues such as racial harmony could be more effective than even the best-intended national government programs.

Yet Reagan was not unacquainted with the bleaker aspects of American life, or life in general. He might be viewed as having a "second innocence" or "second naiveté"—not the innocence of ignorance, but a disciplined approach that used optimism to *encourage* himself and others to achieve their potential.

Like his idol Franklin Roosevelt, Reagan transformed his characteristic optimism into an indispensable part of his leadership. Another leader admired by Reagan, Dwight Eisenhower, candidly talked about the role of disciplined optimism in several lines deleted from the final version of his war memoir, *Crusade in Europe:* "Optimism and pessimism are infectious and they spread more rapidly from the head downward than in any other direction. [Optimism] has a most extraordinary effect upon all with whom [the commander] comes in contact. With this clear realization, I firmly determined that my mannerisms and speech in public would always reflect the cheerful certainty of victory—that any pessimism and discouragement I might ever feel would be reserved for my pillow."

Reagan's confidence in the future was unbounded; he "[took] inspiration from the past; like most Americans, I live for the future." His confidence was based upon his faith in God; indeed, the word is derived from the Latin, "with faith." From his mother he imbibed the view "that God has a plan for everyone and that seemingly random twists of fate are all part of His plan . . . in the end, everything worked out for the best." His faith in God's plan was with him from his beginnings in Tampico and Dixon, Illinois, through trials and achievements he could never have foreseen, into the hearts and history of his nation.

EMPATHY, GRACE, AND CHARM

As in other areas, Reagan credited his acting background with his development of empathy:

> After a while, whenever I read a new script, I'd automatically try first to understand what made that particular human being tick by trying to put myself in his place. The process, called empathy, is not bad training for someone who goes into politics (or any other calling). By developing a knack for putting yourself in someone else's shoes, it helps you relate better to others and

perhaps understand why they think as they do, even though they come from a background much different from yours.

This character trait underlies the related qualities that marked Reagan—grace and charm—and was the source of his ability to focus on audiences. The evident nature of his personal empathy was also a key component of his inclusive vision and encouraged the trust that was reposed in him by millions.

To a degree rarely observed today, Reagan demonstrated grace in dealing with political opponents. Early in his presidency, exercising an authority granted by Congress in 1978, he personally presented a gold medal to Mrs. Ethel Kennedy in honor of her late husband, Robert F. Kennedy. In 1985 he spoke at the home of Senator Edward Kennedy to raise funds for the John F. Kennedy Library Foundation. In an eloquent tribute to the late president, he recalled "the man himself and what his life meant to our country and our times, particularly to the history of this century."

Perhaps most revealing was his participation in the dedication of the Carter museum in October 1986. Given Carter's slashing personal attacks on Reagan and his manifest resentment at his 1980 defeat, this was a delicate situation. Former press aide Larry Speakes recalled that during the flight to Atlanta, the Reagans set the tone for the event, telling him, "We have made up our minds that no matter what happens, we're going to be gracious."

During his speech, looking directly at Carter, Reagan spoke not of his erstwhile political opponent, but of the dedicated man who preceded him in the Oval Office: "Your countrymen have vivid memories of your time in the White House still. They see you working in the Oval Office at your desk with an air of intense concentration, repairing to a quiet place to receive the latest word on the hostages you did so much to free, or studying in your hideaway office for the meeting at Camp David that would mark such a breakthrough for peace in the Middle East."

Carter responded: "I think I now understand more clearly than I ever had before why you won in November 1980, and I lost."

Reagan's grace was not limited to celebrities. A characteristic example occurred prior to his presidency, when he was a professional public speaker. When a charitable fundraising event in rural Iowa did not meet expectations because of a blizzard, he sat down and wrote a personal check to repay his fee. As governor, he invited a young picketer into his office, concerned about her discomfort in the Sacramento heat.

In the midst of a critical arms control negotiation in Geneva with Soviet general secretary Gorbachev, Reagan made sure he dealt with an unforeseen matter of some urgency to a young acquaintance:

> When Nancy and I returned to our bedroom after dinner, I took one look at a glass aquarium in the room and said, "Oh, lordy."
>
> The children who normally lived in the house had asked me to feed their goldfish. I'd done it, but one of the fish was dead. Maybe I hadn't fed the fish enough, or maybe I had fed it too much. Whatever the reason, it had died on my watch and I felt responsible for it. I asked our staff to put the dead fish into a box and take it to a pet store in Geneva to see whether they could find one exactly like it. Luckily, they found two that matched, and I put them in the tank and wrote a letter to the children to let them know what had happened.

He made certain that James Brady, the widely admired aide who was disabled during the 1981 assassination attempt on Reagan, kept the title of White House press secretary throughout his presidency. When exceptionally cold weather cost marching bands their opportunity to perform at his second inaugural, he made a point of going to an arena to thank them personally and listen to some of their music.

Peggy Noonan has recounted the story of an elderly woman, Frances Green, who was rebuffed at the guard station as she approached the White House. Mrs. Green, a woman of modest means, had traveled all the way from California to meet the president, apparently mistaking an elaborate fundraising solicitation for a personal invitation. When another, more worldly visitor overheard her plight, he notified Reagan's staff and arranged a White House tour for her on the next day.

During the tour, Mrs. Green walked past the Oval Office, hoping for a glimpse of the chief executive on what had become an especially trying day. Nonetheless, as if he had no greater priority, Reagan waved her in. Noonan writes:

> This is why Reagan is Reagan. He knows Mrs. Green is a little old lady all by herself in the world, she's no one, with nothing to give him, and Reagan is behind his desk, and he rises and calls out, "Frances!" He says, "Those darn computers, they fouled up again! If I'd known you were coming I would have come out there to get you myself." He asked her to sit down and they talked about California, and he gave her a lot of time, and if you say on a day like that it was time wasted, there are a lot of people who'd say, Oh no it wasn't. No it wasn't.

DISCIPLINE

Howard Baker describes Reagan as "the most disciplined person I ever saw." This began with his health. Presidents like other executives must take special care of their personal health—be "wise and prudent athletes," as Woodrow Wilson, himself physically ruined in office, urged. Reagan more than met this criterion. He generally kept regular hours, adhering strictly to his daily schedule. Even as president, particularly after the attempt on his life, he followed a strict exercise regimen. He maintained a healthy diet that excluded smoking and only occasionally included beverages with caffeine. Perhaps because of his father's alcoholism, he was a light drinker whose taste ran to red wine and occasional screwdrivers. Martin Anderson observed that he took care of his health in the way all of us know we should; the difference was that he actually did it.

Another area where he showed great discipline was in his public utterances. Reagan was a skilled storyteller who loved to please an audience; like Franklin Roosevelt he also enjoyed talking. At various times in his career, undisciplined speech had proved costly. Premature talk in the Warner Brothers dining room may have enabled others to misappropriate a movie concept. When he was governor, a light quip on a radio show during a California campaign on a tax limitation initiative he strongly supported was used by opponents to help ensure its defeat. Later his telling of an ethnic joke on a bus with reporters in the 1980 campaign caused a minor furor. As president, he was generally very disciplined, even in off-the-record discussions in which journalists were committed not to report his comments.

CONSTANCY AND PERSEVERANCE

Perseverance—the persistent adherence to a single course of action in the face of any and all obstacles—is, rightly, a generally admired trait. It is important to note, however, that such determination may be applied in ways that are good or bad, creative or destructive, courageous or self-regarding. For example, Bill Clinton's strongest demonstrations of persistence and durability have been occasioned by revelations bringing his courage and judgment into serious question. One recalls his 1992 presidential campaign in New Hampshire, where he doggedly continued to campaign even as the public learned about his dissembling concerning his draft eligibility and status as a young man.

At various points in his life, Reagan combined courage with determination to persevere in very difficult circumstances. In his 1976 primary challenge to an incumbent president, he faced the combined power of the president's control of the party apparatus and the executive branch. In short order, Reagan's campaign faltered after successive defeats in early primary states; it was in debt and its prospects were, at best, limited. Even his own staff was losing heart, with some not hiding their expectation that Reagan's effort was doomed.

He surprised friend and foe by electing to stay in the race. Martin Anderson recalls the critical meeting, held in Reagan's hotel suite in Wisconsin on March 23, 1976: "Reagan was quiet—the whole room was quiet, for what seemed like endless minutes—before he spoke. 'OK, we'll do it. . . . I'm going to take this all the way to the convention in Kansas City, and I'm going even if I lose every damn primary between now and then.'"

As the nation watched, this former movie actor—who appeared to have had an effortless ascent from small-town penury to Hollywood stardom and then to national political prominence—persevered in the face of the public challenges and personal indignities that make up election campaigns. In the end, though he fell just short of his party's nomination, Reagan's demonstrated perseverance showcased many of his leadership qualities.

That same perseverance would mark his approach to the economic challenges of his first term as president and through the many ups and downs of his ultimately successful policies toward the Soviet Union. It was demonstrated with poignancy in 1987. Reagan was 76 years old, heading toward the end of his second term in office. In the course of one year, he encountered continuing criticism and distraction arising from the Iran-Contra scandal, the stock market collapsed, his beloved wife had a mastectomy, and his mother-in-law died. Nonetheless, Reagan persevered, his leadership recovered, and he left office with the unmatched affection of the American people, as well as many others around the world.

Related to perseverance is constancy. Reagan kept commitments. A representative example arose in the 1976 primary campaign. Following a remarkable comeback, Reagan arrived at the Republican National Convention in Kansas City with an outside possibility of wresting the nomination from President Ford. As a bold stroke to attract delegates, he broke tradition and announced his choice for vice president in advance of the presidential selection.

At the convention, Reagan's choice of Pennsylvania senator Richard Schweiker occasioned at least as much consternation among long-time Reagan backers as potential conversions among Ford backers. Former senator Paul Laxalt, one of Reagan's closest supporters then and later, recounts Schweiker's offer to leave the ticket: "The senator said to Governor Reagan, 'I think I've become a liability to this ticket and respectfully request to be replaced.' Ronald Reagan, facing a desperate situation, could have taken the easy route and granted the senator's request. Instead, without hesitating, he said, 'No, Dick. We came to Kansas City together and we're going to leave together.'"

HUMILITY

Given the immense self-confidence and self-discipline associated with leadership at high levels, some might not immediately recognize humility as an important personal trait for leaders. Perhaps the best explanation, on the highest authority, is that of Dwight Eisenhower in the immediate aftermath of the Allied victory in Europe in 1945: "Humility must always be the portion of any man who receives acclaim earned in the blood of his followers and the sacrifices of his friends."

Reagan's humility was a defining characteristic long before he achieved the presidency. In his 1969 eulogy for his friend, fellow actor Robert Taylor, he recognized Taylor as "a truly modest man" of many virtues, "above all, an inner humility." Reagan had a sharp awareness of the unpredictability of human affairs. In his autobiography he recalled an experience during an early career breakthrough. Reagan had received a coveted lead role in a favored film. One of his first tasks was to be fitted for the costumes. As he waited he noticed discarded costumes for the same role, emblazoned with the name of another actor. Reagan reminded himself, "That can happen to me some day."

Even as president, surrounded by staff whose job it was to attend to his every need, Reagan maintained a personal modesty. He often printed addresses by hand on envelopes to avoid asking too much of his secretary; he cleaned up water he spilled at the hospital during his recovery from his 1981 shooting to avoid troubling the nurses; he was uncomfortable disrupting church services with the security checks that were imposed on other people when he attended.

Reagan found warm displays of public support during his presidency to be "humbling," and they led him to pray that he would not let the people down. He understood the necessity of maintaining humility in a leadership role: "otherwise the power goes to your head, and the history books are littered with such unsavory people."

DISTANCE AND DIGNITY OF OFFICE

Ronald Reagan was at once warmly approachable yet unmistakably distant. It is often observed that he had few close personal friends. Even his wife, Nancy, with whom he shared a remarkable closeness, has been quoted as saying, "You can get just so far to Ronnie, and then something happens."

Whatever the effect of his distance in his personal life, it was unquestionably a factor in his working life and leadership style. In his early autobiography—*Where's the Rest of Me?*—he relates his first experience in Hollywood. After being filmed for a screen test, Reagan prepared to return to Des Moines:

> Then they told me it would be several days before Mr. Warner could see the film and, of course, I would stick around, to which I said, "No, I will be on the train tomorrow—me and the [Chicago] Cubs are going home."
>
> They were unbelieving, but I was adamant. It was only on the train that suddenly the horrified feeling came over me that maybe I had blown the whole thing. . . . (Actually I had done, through ignorance, the smartest thing it was possible to do. Hollywood just loves people who don't need Hollywood.)

As Reagan assumed increasing levels of responsibility, one always had a sense that there were many things Reagan would not do either to attain or maintain any particular leadership position. In no sense did he need it.

When he thought of the presidency, or the White House itself, Reagan never forgot that he had been granted "only temporary custody" of entities that belonged to the American people. As he came to personify his vision, he nonetheless did not confuse himself with the institution of the presidency. He insisted on a sense of dignity of the office, a high standard that might not always be reached but would always be sought. As one discrete but unmistakable example: Even in hot weather, Reagan would continue to wear his suitcoat in the Oval Office. Howard Baker, no stranger to the White House, concludes that Reagan was "the most *presidential* president I have ever known."

His sense of setting high standards and upholding the dignity of office was also reflected in things he would *not* do. For example, during the Iran-Contra affair, he declined to assert executive privilege and other legal mechanisms designed to limit public disclosure. Even though it would have been within his legal rights to do so, his view of the presidency required a higher standard than that of a defensive politician, much less a prospective criminal defendant. Similarly, Reagan would not grant pardons to administration officials caught in that scandal, even though he may have felt great personal sympathy for them. Reagan did not pick up the telephone in the Oval Office and ask potential contributors for campaign money. Unlike one of his successors, he never publicly discussed his preferences in undergarments.

One of the potential benefits of distance is perspective. Reagan brought an unusual perspective both from his unconventional career path and from the fact that he had succeeded to the highest level in another field of endeavor. He also made certain that he spent a good amount of time out of the White House and away from Washington. According to Lou Cannon, Reagan spent 345 days of his presidency at his California ranch.

As president, he also maintained perspective by keeping a personal diary of events. Keeping a diary can be a useful exercise, reminding one of the larger picture being painted through the light brush strokes left by daily small events during crowded hours.

It may be that Reagan's distance shaded into problematic detachment in some cases, and perhaps he could have avoided disappointing some of his immediate staff had he been better able to reach them at a personal level. Nonetheless, as we have seen, it can also have positive consequences in terms of leadership and management. For leaders of great enterprises, distance approaches another issue: mystery. Charles de Gaulle, considering military leadership, urged, "In the designs, the demeanor, and the mental operations of a leader there must always be a 'something' which others cannot altogether fathom, which puzzles them, stirs them, and rivets their attention."

At the highest levels of leadership an individual must be willing to stand alone. This does not suggest physical isolation, but a manifestly self-contained personality. Reagan always rejected the view that in his case the presidency was a staggering burden. As with Eisenhower, one does not find photographs of Reagan in anguish as he made consequential decisions. Nonetheless, de Gaulle's summation of the personal costs of leadership at the highest level may still be apt:

> Aloofness, character, and the personification of greatness, these qualities it is that surround with prestige those who are prepared to carry a burden which is too heavy for lesser mortals. The price they have to pay for leadership is unceasing self-discipline, the constant taking of risks, and a perpetual inner struggle. The degree of suffering involved varies according to the temperament of the individual. . . . The leader who keeps himself, perforce, in isolation from his fellows, turns his back upon those simpler pleasures which are the gift of unconstraint, familiar intercourse, and, even, of friendship. . . . The choice must be made, and it is a hard one: whence the vague sense of melancholy which hangs about the skirts of majesty, in things no less than people. One day somebody said to Napoleon, as they were looking at an old and noble monument: "How sad it is!" "Yes," came the reply, "as sad as greatness."

REAGAN ON LEADERSHIP: REAGAN'S PERSONAL TRAITS

- *Courage*. Reagan consistently demonstrated various types of courage throughout his life. In ways large and small this demonstrated a heedlessness of self that is a key to high-level leadership.

- *Authenticity.* Reagan used his acting skills to effectively communicate his authenticity. This was a critical component of his ability to earn the trust of others.

- *Confidence.* Reagan's religious faith gave him a durable confidence and undergirded his characteristic optimism.

- *Empathy.* Reagan's high degree of empathy—honed from his work as an actor—was a key component of his ability to communicate effectively by focusing on his audience.

- *Discipline.* From his focus on his audience as a speaker to his diet and exercise routine, Reagan demonstrated ongoing discipline.

- *Perseverance* and *Constancy*.

- *Humility*.

- *Distance.* Reagan's unusual combination of approachability and distance was a key feature of his leadership approach. He strove to protect the dignity of the public offices he held. He maintained a strong sense of perspective on his work and was a uniquely self-contained personality.

EPILOGUE

IN THE ELOQUENT words of George Shultz, Ronald Reagan as we knew him is no longer with us. Nonetheless, his leadership remains the standard by which many judge those currently on the scene.

In his first presidential inaugural address Reagan turned America's attention to its heroes. First he spoke of those whom we remember with monuments, such as George Washington, "[a] man of humility who came to greatness reluctantly." Then he turned to the thousands of heroes of everyday American life, exemplified by Martin Treptow, "who left his job in a small town barbershop in 1917 [World War I] to go to France with the famed Rainbow Division."

Reagan, who rose from a small Midwest town to the height of world leadership, never needed a monument, nor forgot that America's greatness is built on the millions of individuals who demonstrate heroism in their own lives. His leadership and accomplishments did not separate him from the people he sought to serve; they brought him closer to them.

Contemporary Americans have sometimes felt disappointment in leaders who have brought doubt or even disrepute to institutions as beloved as the United Way and as sacred as the White House. Some in leadership positions seem to regard the enforced isolation provided them in large institutions as an opportunity for personal gratification rather than as a sanctuary from which they can attain the perspective needed to rise to the level of events. While Reagan came to personify his vision with remarkable consequences for his leadership, he never confused himself with the institution of the presidency. He constantly reminded himself and others that even though he resided in the White House, it was not *his* house. He never forgot that he held it in trust for those he served, and he prayed that he would be worthy of the responsibility.

Some of the unconventional aspects of Reagan's leadership and management style may have resulted from his career as a professional actor. His powerful concentration on the issue at hand, and his apparent awareness of coworkers only in the context of the projects in which they worked together, added to an impression of remoteness felt by some others accustomed to the rhythms and customs of the large private and public organizations of the postwar era. What was unconventional in Reagan's time may become more common in the future. Some management experts, including Tom Peters and Anthony Sampson, now suggest that the film crew model—where a group of independent specialists is assembled for the purpose of efficiently creating a specified product within a limited time period, and is then disbanded—may become a fixture in the emerging Information Age economy.

The most important parts of Reagan's leadership approach are timeless and applicable in virtually any setting. His articulation of and adherence to a compelling vision is the single most important element. His management practices succeeded because they were built around accomplishing his vision. His communications skills enabled him ultimately to embody his vision. His personal character traits combined to demonstrate to one and all that he put achievement of his vision above concern for himself.

When people are asked to recall their first impression upon seeing Reagan in person they almost invariably talk about how "big" he was. This is curious, because while he was indeed larger than average, he was by no means a physical giant. It was his powerful spirit that would fill up a room, then a nation, ultimately much of the world. Reagan is now in physical decline, but the shadow cast by his spirit is lengthening. In the many languages spoken in our world—from China to the Middle East to Russia to the Americas—the word "Reagan" now means one thing: leadership.

SOURCE NOTES

Introduction

"I was not at my best" and other references to President Carter and his actions are from his narrative of his final day of office in his book *Keeping Faith: Memoirs of a President,* New York: Bantam Books (1982), pp. 1–14, except as otherwise noted; "No, sir, I'm not" quoted in Johnson, p. 26; "Does that mean I have to get up?" Deaver, pp. 98–99, and also interview with Michael K. Deaver, November 25, 1997; "poised for takeoff" Johnson, pp. 38–39; "he had not slept all night" Deaver, pp. 99, 100; "I think it is outrageous" quoted in Deaver, p. 100; "I wished he had had the chance" AL, p. 227; "an affront" AL, p. 225; "Watching the sun break through" AL, p. 226; "an outstanding or above-average president" Anderson, p. xxviii; *"How the hell does he do it?"* AL, p. 276 (emphasis added); "Ronald Reagan had very little" Schieffer and Gates, p. 374; "There was no design for leadership" Regan, p. 217; "one of the largest margins in United States history" Anderson, p. xxvi; "No one is that lucky" Anderson, p. xxvii; "bird shot" AL, p. 276.

PART ONE: LEADERSHIP

"do the greatest things" "Ronald Reagan," *Biography,* A&E, February 1996.

Chapter One

"a conviction, even a passion" Bennis and Nanus, p. xi; "clearly desirable, and energizing" Bennis and Nanus, p. 95; "Reaganism" interview with Dr. Martin Anderson, October 29, 1997; "I know of no greater force on earth" AL, p. 28; "value found only in family and faith" remarks and question-and-answer session with students at Moscow State University, May 31, 1988; "not powerful enough to replace them" remarks to the American Conservative Union Banquet, Washington, D.C., February 6, 1977; "entrepreneurial drive of the American people" address to the Republican National Convention, August 17, 1992; "the rewards of their individual labor" address to the Republican National Convention, p. 205; "get the big contract and be home free" remarks at a luncheon for Representative Connie Mack, Miami, Florida, June 29, 1988; "the backbone of our country" remarks to National Charity Awards Dinner, Phoenix, Arizona, January 23, 1992; "do the right things for themselves and others" for example, see AL, pp. 28, 46; "if things went wrong for you" AL, p. 27; "There is a role for churches and temples" remarks on Private Sector Initiatives at White House luncheon for National Religious Leaders, April 13, 1982; "reduced their importance and their budget" AL, p. 69; "that word is 'freedom'" remarks at the annual convention of National Religious Broadcasters, February 4, 1985; "come to live in America and become an American" remarks at the presentation ceremony for the Presidential Medal of Freedom, January 19, 1989; "with faith in their Maker and their future" remarks at the National Prayer Breakfast, February 4, 1982; "I've spoken of the shining city" Farewell Address to the Nation, January 11, 1989; "open to all peoples, everywhere" remarks at the National Prayer Breakfast, February 4, 1988; "every one of us . . . has something to offer" remarks and question-and-answer session with students at Moscow State University, May 31, 1988; "made America the envy of all mankind" address to the nation, July 27, 1981; "silent form of socialism" AL, p. 120; "continue to move toward socialism" Hayek, p. 7; "Regimes planted by bayonets do not take root" address to the members of the British Parliament, Palace of Westminster, June 8, 1982; "expansionism of the Communist states" AL, p. 556; "morality is a necessary spring of popular government" remarks and question-and-answer session with students at Moscow State University, May 31, 1988; "guided by an inner personal code of morality" remarks at Eisenhower College fund-raiser, Washington, D.C., October 14, 1969; "constant threat of nuclear war" AL, p. 550; "we only aim to hit other missiles" AL, p. 549 (emphasis in original); "fight for peace in the nuclear age" AL, p. 709; "your words mean something" SMM, p. 85; "there are simple answers—there are just not easy ones" inaugural address as governor of California, Sacramento, January 5, 1967; "offer a solution everybody can understand" Powell, p. 395; "rediscovery of our values and common sense" Farewell Address to the Nation, January 11, 1989; "his vision encompassed the unprecedented changes" interview with Dr. Kevin Starr, December 16, 1997; "the country of tomorrow" address to the Republican National Convention, Houston, Texas, August 17, 1992.

Chapter Two

"His most outstanding leadership quality" quoted in Hannaford, p. 40; "I meant what I said" AL p. 283; "70 percent . . . went on strike" (and other facts in this section) from AL, pp. 282–283; "we had to do what was right" SMM, p. 85; "will be terminated" SMM, p. 86; "back up his principles" Professor Richard Pipes, quoted in Meese, p. 18n; "We didn't ask anybody" AL, pp. 457–458; "speculation by outside observers" Shultz, p. 323; "coalition with at least one other country" Shultz, p. 329; "another Vietnam" AL, p. 451; "killed 241 marines" AL, p. 453; "informed rather than consulted" Shultz, p. 335; "Reagan felt he could not tell her" AL, pp. 454–455; "none of us . . . slept well" AL, p. 455; "the man with a rifle" quoted in Shultz, p. 345; "the mad clown of Tripoli" AL, p. 511; "affiliated organizations across the world" AL, p. 280; "ordered them to go forward" AL, p. 281; "Yes sir" AL, p. 289; "retaliation by the United States" AL, p. 511; "responsible for the bombing" AL, p. 518; "Libyan terrorist network" AL, p. 519; "no sanctuary anywhere" address to the nation on the U.S. air strike against Libya; "in retaliation for the raid" AL, p. 520; "a U.S.–U.S.S.R. summit" AL, p. 664; "potential for civilian losses" AL, p. 518; "the direction you choose" Bennis and Nanus, pp. 44–45; "clemency to a convicted murderer" Cannon, *Reagan,* p. 167n; "with his Russian counterpart" AL, p. 674.

Chapter Three

"Before I took up" remarks to the National Chamber Foundation, November 17, 1988; "He'll sit here" quoted in Neustadt, p. 10 (emphasis in original); "I'd matched wits" AL, p. 171; "an interview prior to the

Reykjavik summit" Michael Putzel, "Reagan Compares His Union Bargaining Days in Hollywood With US-Soviet Talks," Associated Press, October 9, 1986; "Reagan worked on his own schedule" for example, see AL, p. 601; "back at the table" AL, p. 587; "once the negotiations start" Cannon, "Fresh Tests Awaiting Negotiator-in-Chief," *Washington Post,* March 28, 1983; "get *all* you want" AL, p. 637 (emphasis in original); "perhaps even to himself" Anderson, p. 284; "commitments to buy American grain" AL, p. 675; "wanting to reduce nuclear weapons" AL, p. 297; "listen to what they are offering" Cannon, *Reagan,* p. 154; "even your own bottom line" AL, p. 286; "or humiliate him" AL, p. 637; "hard to do in such situations" quoted in Hannaford, p. 69; "a personal approach to Gorbachev" AL, pp. 12–16, "days of my presidency" AL, p. 675; "performed so well at that moment" Kenneth Adelman, transcript of interview on C-SPAN *Booknotes,* October 22, 1989; "talk about what you're negotiating" Helen Thomas, "Reagan: U.S. Still Negotiating With Noriega," United Press International, May 17, 1988; "Reagan would often delegate" for example, see Cannon, "Fresh Tests"; "one tough son of a bitch" quoted in Winik, p. 213; "alone and in private" AL, p. 637; "louse up the agreement" AL, p. 634; "highest possible batting average" AL, p. 171; "never got used to it" AL, p. 171; "a complete victory" Boyarsky, p. 124; "achieved a substantial victory" Anderson, p. 285; "Gorbachev agreed" AL, p. 701; "furthering the original Reagan objective" Meg Greenfield, "How Does Reagan Decide?" *Washington Post,* February 15, 1984.

Chapter Four

The von Moltke and de Robeck quotations are from Liddell Hart, p. 14; "I began to realize" Liddell Hart, p. 18; "carted me off to an institution" AL, p. 59 (emphasis in original); "lead me into the movies" AL, p. 60; "in the new radio industry" AL, pp. 60–61; "write a screenplay" AL, pp. 90–91; "public demand for his entry" for example, see Cannon, *Reagan,* p. 229; "no more money can be spent" quoted in Moynihan, p. 273; "Nobody wanted a second-class army" AL, p. 235; "by 1984 at the latest" AL, p. 235; "Nor could America regain confidence" AL, p. 333; "recessions increased the deficit" AL, p. 312; "too much spending" AL, p. 336; "the problem was structural" see Anderson, pp. 182–188, for a detailed recounting of the case for structural reform; "resulting in significant savings" AL, p. 341; "Two hundred million, they couldn't" AL, pp. 182–183; "What then will be left to cut?" Moynihan, p. 158; "driven out of existence" Moynihan, p. 158; "strong evidence to the contrary" interview with Dr. Martin Anderson, October 29, 1997; "proposing new spending programs" quoted in E. J. Dionne, "Reagan Debt Legacy: His Trap for Democrats?" *New York Times,* December 2, 1988; "increases the deficit" see the provocative article, Stan Collender, "We'll Always Have the Deficit (Or Was That Paris?)," *National Journal Cloakroom,* September 2, 1997, for a discussion of the reliance of the statutory budgetary enforcement tools on the existence of the deficit; "perhaps even to himself" Anderson, p. 284; "serendipitous circumstance" for an informed and interesting interpretation of Reagan's decision-making process on the deficit, see Richard E. Neustadt, "Presidents, Politics and Analysis," The Brewster C. Denny Lecture for 1986 at the Graduate School for Public Affairs, University of Washington, May 13, 1986.

Chapter Five

"experience is the greatest teacher" from remarks and question-and-answer session with students at Moscow State University, May 31, 1988; "strong performers who make mistakes" for example, see Bennis and Nanus, pp. 193–194; "the recession was a lagging consequence" for example, see AL, pp. 314–315; "classify the policy as mistaken" was an interpretation related to Reagan's vision of economics, which relied more on microeconomics than macroeconomics, as discussed in Chapter One—see Neustadt, Denny Lecture, for an interpretation imputing similar thoughts to Reagan regarding deficit spending; "Hang tough and stay the course" AL, pp. 589–590 (emphasis added); "even if it cost you some money" SMM, p. 335; "like any other cornered politician" Cannon, p. 684; "A few months ago I told the American people" and the other quotations from Reagan in the remainder of this chapter, unless otherwise noted, are from the speech of March 4, 1987; "support among the American people rose as a result" see Neustadt, *Presidential Power,* for a summary and interpretation of the handling of the Bay of Pigs crisis; "prepared to let him move on" Cannon, p. 738; "the recovery is a success story" Neustadt, p. 279; "More than a quarter of a million casualties" see Hayward, pp. 27–42, and Manchester, pp. 512–589, for background on Churchill's handling of Gallipoli; "millions of his countrymen" see Hayward, pp. 180–181, and Manchester, pp. 791–799, for background on Churchill and the gold standard issue; "I have prayed for them and their loved ones" AL, p. 466; "to prevent a recurrence" AL, p. 466; "I couldn't get my message across" AL, p. 532; "this better thing that *did* happen" AL, p. 21 (emphasis in original); "toehold in Chicago" AL, p. 61; "job with Montgomery Ward" AL, pp. 21, 61; "job as a radio announcer" AL, p. 70; "smoke-filled night-clubs" AL, pp. 124–125; "successful television program" AL, p. 126; "things would work out all right" AL, p. 76; "born four months prematurely," Cannon, p. 227; "containing the barest facts" AL, p. 92; "Michael Korda" article titled "Prompting the President," *New Yorker,* October 6, 1997; "undercuts their self-confidence" Hyatt and Gottlieb, pp. 148, 149–150; "coping with his father's alcoholism" see Cannon, p. 226, Woititz, *Adult Children of Alcoholics,* pp. 7–22; "Reagan's continuing belief in his own innocence" Cannon, p. 226.

Chapter Six

"How about that timing?" quoted in Neustadt, p. 274; *"a clock in his head"* interview with Kenneth L. Khachigian, January 3, 1998 (emphasis added); "Reagan was initially resistant" AL, p. 145; "putting us in an awful spot" AL, pp. 146–147; "he announced pretty much on his own timetable" Nofziger, p. 34; "I'm going to wait as long as I can" remarks and a question-and-answer session with writers for Hispanic religious and labor publications, September 14, 1983; "as silent as a Trappist monk" Walter Shapiro, "At Last Off—and Running," *Newsweek,* February 6, 1984; "put him at a disadvantage" Cannon, *Reagan,* p. 229; "sworn in just after midnight" Nofziger, p. 61; "A head-hunting operation was established" Anderson, p. 198, plus information from interview with Craig L. Fuller, December 8, 1997; "a strategy for the first hundred days" interview with Craig L. Fuller, December 8, 1997; "workaday world of the federal bureaucracy" Anderson, pp. 197–199, plus information from interview with Craig L. Fuller, December 8, 1997; "say some frank things about the Russians" AL, p. 267; "That's what you go for" quoted in Bruce Handy, "It's All About Timing," *Time,* January 12, 1998; "giving his audiences good value" interview with Peter Hannaford, December 9, 1997; "no pale pastel shades" television coverage of the 1976 Republican National Convention, Reagan Library archive; "diagnosed with Alzheimer's disease" AL, p. 94.

PART TWO: MANAGEMENT

Chapter Seven

"in the long run you get more done" address to the nation on the Tower Commission Report, March 4, 1987; "contributes to worthwhile ends" Bennis and Nanus, p. 85 (emphasis in original); "tell them every few minutes what to do" AL, p. 161 (emphasis in original); "a shared and empowering vision of the future" Bennis and Nanus, pp. 84–85; "they knew what he stood for" Noonan, p. 171; "I knew what I had to do" discussion with James W. Fuller, August 26, 1997; "the wrong side of a tapestry" quoted in Bennis and Nanus, p. 35; "strategy will fail if that consensus is missing" Bennis and Nanus, p. 85; "two hours per week to review of appointments" Ann Reilly Dowd, "What Managers Can Learn from Manager Reagan," reprinted in Boyer, p. 61; "left largely to the discretion of the cabinet secretaries" Anderson, p. 199, and also discussion with James W. Fuller, August 26, 1997; "no matter how hard they tried" see Meese, pp. 86–100, for a discussion of the Reagan White House's perception of "The Powers That Be" their administration faced in Washington, D.C.; "it had much greater effect" Meese, p. 34; "challenges in their own bailiwicks" interview with Edwin Meese III, December 11, 1997; "the province of . . . the elected chief executive" Anderson, pp. 224–233 plus information from interviews with Edwin Meese III, December 11, 1997, and with Craig L. Fuller, December 8, 1997; "recent Reagan speeches and actions" interviews with Edwin Meese III, December 11, 1997, with Craig L. Fuller, December 8, 1997, and with Joseph D. Rodota Jr., September 22, 1997; "he rarely gave direct orders" interview with Edwin Meese III, December 11, 1997; "limiting the options of the chief executive" AL, p. 256; "This . . . is dangerous" Regan, p. 142 (emphasis in original); "reading the newspapers" Regan, p. 142; "in line with Reagan's wishes" interview with Edwin Meese III, December 11, 1997; "bedeviled presidential studies for years to come" Newstadt, p. 270; "relying on his complete trust" AL, p. 489; "de facto dismantling of the oversight capacity" discussed in Anderson, pp. 352–369; "there are penalties for failure" George F. Will,

"Question for Reagan: Do You Want to Be President?" *Washington Post*, March 1, 1987.

Chapter Eight

"Effective executives do first things first" Drucker, *The Effective Executive*, p. 100; "it will still not be his own" Drucker, *The Effective Executive*, p. 100; "set priorities and do things one at a time" Anderson, p. 57; "only a President could ultimately resolve" Carter, pp. 577–578 (emphasis added); "discussed personally by the two of us" Carter, pp. 577–578 (emphasis added); "I was not sure how much we had accomplished" Carter, p. 578; "people who get nothing done" Drucker, p. 103; "90 percent of our efforts were on economic growth" quoted in Kolb, pp. 23–24 (emphasis in original); "Johnson, Nixon, Ford, and Carter administrations" Ann Reilly Dowd, "What Managers Can Learn from Manager Reagan," reprinted in Boyer, p. 61; "the urgent over the relevant" Drucker, p. 109.

Chapter Nine

"it is not only nonsense, it is immoral" Drucker, p. 37 (emphasis in original); "anything that can be done by them at all" Drucker, p. 37; "conflicts among his principal advisers" Cannon, p. 94; "emanated unmistakably from the White House itself" Cannon, p. 810; "too closely into contact with action in detail" Churchill, p. 8; "the valleys of direct physical and personal action" Churchill, p. 8; "It's the people around him" O'Neill, p. 357; "decisively, and usually, very wisely" Anderson, p. 290; "to make the effort a success" Regan, pp. 265, 266–267; "intervene and make a change" AL, p. 161; "Reagan might become visibly angry" Anderson, p. 287; "a warmly ruthless man" Anderson, p. 288; "North American Aerospace Defense Command in 1979" for example, see Anderson, pp. 80–99; "a consensus among national opinion leaders" for example, see AL p. 631 (Reagan's private decision to offer SDI technology to the Soviets as part of nuclear arms reduction negotiation); "Why do we need the Federal Reserve?" quoted in Anderson, pp. 250–251; "too many political firefights" Robert J. Samuelson, "The Enigma: Ronald Reagan's Goofy Competence," reprinted in Boyer, p. 279.

Chapter Ten

"They are his specific, everyday tools" Drucker, p. 69; "focus it from the start on contribution" Drucker, pp. 69–70; "ensure that I'd hear all sides" AL, p. 253; "supporting a certain project or program" AL, p. 162; "just brand all the babies" quoted in Anderson, pp. 272–277; "up to me and me alone to make the decision" AL, p. 162; "Well, let's round-table that" interview with Edwin Meese III, December 11, 1997; "confusion and uncertainty in the decision-making process" Kolb, p. 182; "insistence on one-page issue summaries" interview with Edwin Meese III, December 11, 1997; "think the White House was on Sesame Street" Stockman, p. 291; "seemed not to follow their line of reasoning at all" D'Souza, p. 121; "telling stories and talking about something quite different" quoted in Gunther, *Roosevelt in Retrospect,* p. 56; "a poor kid from Dixon, Illinois" Rollins, pp. 108–110 (emphasis in original); "he considered his participation essential to achieving his priorities" for example, see Hannaford, pp. 38–39 (quoting Congressman Tony Coehlo); "Well I was meeting with the president" Noonan, p. 152; "We made so much of those winks" Noonan, p. 181; "personal courage in the face of adversity" Noonan, pp. 249–251.

PART THREE: COMMUNICATION

Chapter Eleven

"How could an actor be president?" AL, p. 393; "*trained* as an actor and a televised spokesman" Neustadt, p. 269 (emphasis added); "speak the truth as I saw it and felt it" SMM, p. 14; "convince himself of the rightness of his ultimate position" interview with William F. Buckley Jr., November 28, 1997; "as the scandal unfolded in November 1986" Cannon, p. 683; "a scripted Reagan performance was missing" Cannon, p. 684; "You also get better at delivering it" SMM, p. 59; "Hall's Mentholyptus" interview with Dr. Martin Anderson, October 29, 1997; "always having a copy of his remarks" AL, p. 248; "make it look easy" interview with Kenneth L. Khachigian, January 3, 1998; "It's quite a jolt" Reagan with Hubler, p. 79; "a devastating effect on public confidence" interview with Peter Hannaford, December 9, 1997; "the president might be filmed amid military weaponry" interview with Michael K. Deaver, November 25, 1997, and also see Deaver, p. 141; "his clothing and demeanor in important settings" interview with Kenneth L. Khachigian, January 3, 1998; "He then demonstrated his preferred approach" interviews with Dr. Martin Anderson, October 29, 1997, and with Peter Hannaford, December 9, 1997; "they just cup your thumb," quoted in Anderson, p. 54; "you can't command all that information" AL, p. 328; "something I had never seen Reagan do" Cannon, p. 542; "gestures had probably become habitual over time" interview with Peter Hannaford, December 9, 1997; "resumed his unmistakable, confident stride" interview with Michael K. Deaver, November 25, 1997; "a permanent change of personality" Dean Acheson, "The Supreme Artist," in *London Observer,* p. 37.

Chapter Twelve

"Talk to your audience" Ronald Reagan, "From the Heart," from Ryan, p. 9 (emphasis added); "He . . . called it his 'little secret' Ryan, p. 9; "How could I connect with all those people" Ryan, p. 9; "talking directly and personally to *them*" AL, p. 247 (emphasis in original); "I try to speak as if I am talking to a group of friends" AL, p. 247; "Reagan liked to have the first rows filled with listeners" interview with Michael K. Deaver, November 25, 1997; "focus on one person while delivering a key line" interview with Kenneth L. Khachigian, January 3, 1998; "allows me to read fine print" AL p. 248; "Reagan wrote in a sort of homemade shorthand" Anderson, pp. 48–52; "memorize every word you wanted to say" AL, p. 130; "twenty minutes to be the maximum people should be expected to sit" Noonan, *Simply Speaking,* p. 9; "learn about the issues that were on people's minds" AL, p. 152; "the most important audience suggestions and reactions" AL, p. 129; "We'll just stay and do this until we're finished" interview with Peter Hannaford, December 9, 1997; "theater of the mind" AL, p. 59; "his idol, Franklin Roosevelt" Deaver, p. 37; "the audience represented by the small lens of the camera" Brown and Brown, p. 19; "take it into our own hands" acceptance speech at Republican National Convention, Detroit, Michigan, August 15, 1980.

Chapter Thirteen

"Reagan was his own best speechwriter" interview with Dr. Martin Anderson, October 29, 1997; "his basic philosophy wasn't exactly a secret" Noonan, p. 75; "then I tell them what I told them" AL, p. 247; "Use simple language" AL, p. 246; "An example is better than a sermon" AL, p. 246; "that dollar of 1960 will be worth a quarter" address to the nation on the economy, February 5, 1981; "reach the moon and back two or three times" Hannaford, p. 107; "as if the issue of the whole struggle depended on me alone" inaugural address, January 20, 1981; "trying to figure out where the angel kissed you" AL, p. 377; "exercised some license with the supporting facts" see Cannon, pp. 98–100; "he would not hesitate to . . . rewrite something himself if necessary" interview with Kenneth L. Khachigian, January 3, 1998.

Chapter Fourteen

"you take it in stride" AL, p. 393; "that's why I'm running" AL, p. 150; "never held *any* job before he became a senator" AL, p. 151 (emphasis in original); "the prospect of a Californian in the White House" AL, p. 209; "He took a similar approach to questions about his age" AL, p. 209; "senility factor" AL, p. 328; "what my answer might be to such a question" AL, p. 329; "Where's the rest of me?" Nofziger, pp. 38–39; "persuaded not to abandon the nascent candidacy" Nofziger, pp. 41–42; "quite sophisticated in responding to criticism" AL, p. 150; "Pat wouldn't say anything like that" quoted in Johnson, p. 81; "The reporters roared with laughter" Hannaford, p. 189, and also interview with Kirk West, September 23, 1997; "it was six o'clock" AL, pp. 250–251; "often played to bad reviews" interview with Douglas L. Bailey, December 5, 1997.

PART FOUR: SELF-MANAGEMENT

"But all the world will clamor for it" De Gaulle, p. 46; "Life is one indivisible whole" quoted in Covey, Merrill, and Merrill, p. 121.

Chapter Fifteen

"a word derived from the Latin" *The American Heritage Dictionary of the English Language, 3rd ed.;* "a oneness, primarily with self but also with life" Covey, pp. 195–196 (emphasis in original); "threats of violence and facial disfigurement" AL, p. 108; "not adjusting his plans in response to threats" see, for example, Nofziger, pp. 63–64, 70–71; "two o'clock in the morning courage" toast from Prime Minister Thatcher at the dinner honoring the president, February 27, 1981; "I hope you're a Republican" AL, pp. 259–263; "where I can see the air I'm breathing" Deaver, p. 23; "shortly after the assassination attempt" address at commencement exercises at the University of Notre Dame, May 17, 1981; "keep his own name" AL, p. 83; "the picture didn't ring any bells" AL, p. 138; "the part he played was Ronald Reagan" Noonan, p. 163; "second innocence" this concept is from Maslow, p. 245; "Optimism and pessimism are infectious" quoted from Ambrose, p. 7 (brackets from Ambrose); "like most Americans, I live for the future" address to the Republican National Convention, Houston, Texas, August 17, 1992; "in the end, everything worked out for the best" AL, pp. 20–21; "from a background much different from yours" AL, p. 42; "personally presented a gold medal" remarks on presenting the Robert F. Kennedy Medal to Mrs. Ethel Kennedy, June 5, 1981; "particularly to the history of this century" remarks at a fund-raising reception for the John F. Kennedy Library Foundation, June 24, 1985; "why you won in November 1980" recounted in Speakes, p. 104, "wrote a personal check to repay his fee" Deaver, p. 138; "he invited a young picketer into his office" quoted in Hannaford, p. 145; "Maybe I hadn't fed the fish enough" AL, p. 640; "James Brady . . . kept the title of White House press secretary" AL, p. 488; "listen to some of their music" AL, p. 331; "Those darn computers, they fouled up again!" from Noonan, in Wilson, pp. 219–221; "the most disciplined person I ever saw" interview with Howard H. Baker Jr., December 9, 1997; "he was a light drinker" interview with Michael K. Deaver, November 25, 1997; "the difference was that he actually did it" interview with Martin Anderson, October 29, 1997; "Premature talk in the Warner Brothers dining room" AL, pp. 90–91; "a light quip on a radio show" Cannon, *Reagan*, p. 190; "his telling of an ethnic joke on a bus" Deaver, p. 77; "As president, he was generally very disciplined" see, for example, observations of Fred Barnes, quoted in Hannaford, pp. 15–17; "even if I lose every damn primary between now and then" Anderson, p. 43; "We came to Kansas City together and we're going to leave together" quoted in Hannaford, p. 95; "acclaim earned in the blood of his followers" quoted in Ambrose, p. 7; "above all, an inner humility" SMM, pp. 46–50; "That can happen to me some day" AL, p. 92; "avoid asking too much of his secretary" Noonan, p. 179; "to avoid troubling the nurses" Noonan, p. 15; "he was uncomfortable disrupting church services" interview with Howard H. Baker Jr., December 9, 1997; "pray that he would not let the people down" AL, p. 252; "history books are littered with such unsavory people" AL, p. 199; "You can get just so far to Ronnie" quoted in Cannon, p. 228; "Hollywood just loves people who don't need Hollywood" Reagan with Hubler, pp. 67–68; "entities that belonged to the American people" AL, p. 721; "Reagan would continue to wear his suitcoat in the Oval Office" Deaver, p. 143; "the most *presidential* president I have ever known" interview with Howard H. Baker Jr., December 9, 1997; "stirs them, and rivets their attention" De Gaulle, p. 58; "as sad as greatness" De Gaulle, pp. 65–66.

Key

AL—*An American Life* (Reagan)
Cannon—*President Reagan: The Role of a Lifetime*
Noonan—*What I Saw At the Revolution*
SMM—*Speaking My Mind* (Reagan)
Other items refer to authors of volumes in Bibliography.

SELECT BIBLIOGRAPHY

Ambrose, Stephen E. (ed.). 1990. *The Wisdom of Dwight D. Eisenhower: Quotations from Ike's Speeches and Writings, 1939–1969.* New Orleans: Eisenhower Center.

Anderson, Martin. 1990. *Revolution: The Reagan Legacy.* Stanford, CA: Hoover Institution Press.

Bass, Bernard M. 1985. *Leadership and Performance Beyond Expectations.* New York: Free Press.

Bennis, Warren. 1989. *On Becoming a Leader.* Reading, MA: Addison-Wesley.

Bennis, Warren, and Burt Nanus. 1997 (1985). *Leaders: Strategies for Taking Charge.* New York: HarperBusiness.

Boyarsky, Bill. 1981. *Ronald Reagan: His Life and Rise to the Presidency.* New York: Random House.

Boyer, Paul (ed.). 1990. *Reagan as President: Contemporary Views of the Man, His Politics, and His Policies.* Chicago: Dee.

Brown, Edmund G. (Pat), and Bill Brown. 1976. *Reagan: The Political Chameleon.* New York: Praeger.

Burns, James MacGregor. 1979. *Leadership.* New York: Harper Torchbooks.

Cannon, Lou. 1991. *President Reagan: The Role of a Lifetime.* New York: Simon & Schuster.

Cannon, Lou. 1982. *Reagan.* New York: Putnam.

Churchill, Winston S. 1991 (1932). *Thoughts and Adventures.* New York: Norton.

Covey, Stephen R., with A. Roger Merrill and Rebecca R. Merrill. 1994. *First Things First.* New York: Fireside.

Covey, Stephen R. 1991. *Principle-Centered Leadership.* New York: Fireside.

Covey, Stephen R. 1990. *The Seven Habits of Highly Effective People: Restoring the Character Ethic*. New York: Fireside.

Dallek, Robert. 1984. *Ronald Reagan: The Politics of Symbolism*. Cambridge, MA: Harvard University Press.

Deaver, Michael K., with Mickey Herskowitz. 1987. *Behind the Scenes*. New York: Morrow.

De Gaulle, Charles. 1960 (1932). *The Edge of the Sword* (Gerard Hopkins, trans.). New York: Criterion.

Donald, David Herbert. 1995. *Lincoln*. New York: Simon & Schuster.

Drucker, Peter F. 1993 (1966). *The Effective Executive*. New York: Harper-Business.

Drucker, Peter F. 1986. *Innovation and Entrepreneurship*. New York: HarperCollins.

Drucker, Peter F. 1985 (1973). *Management*. New York: HarperCollins.

D'Souza, Dinesh. 1997. *Ronald Reagan: How an Ordinary Man Became an Extraordinary Leader*. New York: Free Press.

Evans, Rowland, Jr., and Robert D. Novak. 1981. *The Reagan Revolution*. New York: Dutton.

Gardner, Howard. *Leading Minds*. 1995. New York: Basic Books.

Gunther, John. 1965. *Procession*. New York: HarperCollins.

Gunther, John. 1950. *Roosevelt in Retrospect: A Profile in History*. New York: HarperCollins.

Haig, Alexander. 1984. *Caveat: Realism, Reagan and Foreign Policy*. New York: Macmilllan.

Hannaford, Peter. 1997. *Recollections of Reagan*. New York: Morrow.

Hayek, Fredrich A. 1994 (1944). *The Road to Serfdom*. Chicago: University of Chicago Press.

Hayward, Steven F. 1997. *Churchill on Leadership*. Rocklin, CA: Prima.

Hyatt, Carole, and Linda Gottlieb. 1987. *When Smart People Fail*. New York: Simon & Schuster.

Johnson, Haynes. 1992. *Sleepwalking Through History: America in the Reagan Years*. New York: Anchor.

Liddell Hart, Basil H. 1960 (1954). *Strategy*. New York: Praeger.

London Observer (ed.). 1965. *Churchill by His Contemporaries*. London: Hodder & Stoughton.

Manchester, William. 1983. *The Last Lion: Winston Spencer Churchill, Visions of Glory, 1874–1932*. New York: Little, Brown.

Maraniss, David. 1995. *First in His Class: A Biography of Bill Clinton*. New York: Simon & Schuster.

Maslow, Abraham H. 1986 (1971). *The Farther Reaches of Human Nature*. New York: Penguin.

Meese, Edwin, III. 1992. *With Reagan: The Inside Story*. Washington: Regnery Gateway.

Moynihan, Daniel Patrick. 1988. *Came the Revolution: Argument in the Reagan Era*. Orlando: Harcourt Brace.

Neustadt, Richard E. 1990. *Presidential Power and the Modern Presidents: The Politics of Leadership from Roosevelt to Reagan*. New York: Free Press.

Nofziger, Lyn. 1992. *Nofziger*. Washington, DC: Regnery Gateway.

Noonan, Peggy. 1998. *Simply Speaking: How to Communicate Your Ideas with Style, Substance, and Clarity*. New York: ReganBooks.

Noonan, Peggy. 1991. *What I Saw at the Revolution: A Political Life in the Reagan Era*. New York: Ivy.

O'Neill, Tip, with William Novak. 1987. *Man of the House: The Life and Political Memoirs of Speaker Tip O'Neill*. New York: Random House.

Reagan, Nancy, with William Novak. 1989. *My Turn: The Memoirs of Nancy Reagan*. New York: Random House.

Reagan, Ronald. 1990. *An American Life: The Autobiography*. New York: Simon & Schuster.

Reagan, Ronald. 1989. *Speaking My Mind: Selected Speeches*. New York: Simon & Schuster.

Reagan, Ronald, with Richard G. Hubler. 1965. *Where's the Rest of Me?* New York: Basic Books.

Regan, Donald T. 1988. *For the Record: From Wall Street to Washington*. Orlando: Harcourt Brace.

Rollins, Ed, with Thomas deFrank. 1996. *Bare Knuckles and Back Rooms: My Life in American Politics*. New York: Broadway.

Ryan, Frederick J., Jr. (ed.). 1995. *Ronald Reagan: The Wisdom and Humor of the Great Communicator*. San Francisco: HarperCollins.

Schieffer, Bob, and Gary Paul Gates. 1989. *The Acting President*. New York: Dutton.

Shultz, George P. 1993. *Turmoil and Triumph: My Years as Secretary of State*. New York: Scribner.

Speakes, Larry, with Robert Pack. 1988. *Speaking Out: The Reagan Presidency from Inside the White House*. New York: Scribner.

Sun Tzu. 1988. *The Art of War* (Thomas Clary, trans.). Boston: Shambhala.

Von Damm, Helene. 1988. *At Reagan's Side*. New York: Doubleday.

Will, George F. 1988. *The Morning After: American Successes and Excesses, 1981–1986*. New York: Collier.

Wills, Garry. 1987. *Reagan's America: Innocents at Home*. New York: Doubleday.

Wilson, Robert A. 1996. *Character Above All: Ten Presidents from FDR to George Bush*. New York: Simon & Schuster.

Winik, Jay. 1996. *On the Brink*. New York: Simon & Schuster.

Woititz, Janet G. 1985. *Struggle for Intimacy*. Pompano Beach, Fla.: Health Communications.

Woititz, Janet G. 1983. *Adult Children of Alcoholics*. Pompano Beach, Fla.: Health Communications.

INDEX

About the Author

From 1991–97 James M. Strock served in the cabinet of Governor Pete Wilson as California's first secretary for environmental protection. He previously served as chief law enforcement officer at the U.S. Environmental Protection Agency, as special counsel to the U.S. Senate Environment and Public Works Committee, and as general counsel to the U.S. Office of Personnel Management. He was also a lawyer in private practice.

A graduate of Harvard College (Phi Beta Kappa) and Harvard Law School, Strock served to captain in the U.S. Army Reserve. He has also been a member of the adjunct faculty at the University of Southern California in Los Angeles.

He currently runs a management and public affairs consulting firm in San Francisco and is a director on several corporate and non-profit boards.

Strock has published articles in numerous national and foreign publications and is a frequent public speaker. His e-mail address is *jamesmstrock@msn.com*.